Brain-Powered Lessons to Engage All Learners

Author

LaVonna Roth, M.S.Ed.

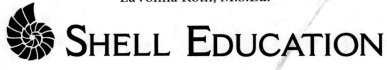

SHELL EDUCATION

Publishing Credits

Robin Erickson, *Production Director*; Lee Aucoin, *Creative Director*;
Timothy J. Bradley, *Illustration Manager*; Emily R. Smith, M.A.Ed., *Editorial Director*;
Jennifer Wilson, *Editor*; Evelyn Garcia, M.A.Ed., *Editor*; Amber Goff, *Editorial Assistant*;
Grace Alba Le, *Designer*; Corinne Burton, M.A.Ed., *Publisher*

Image Credits

p. 38, 111 istockphoto; all other images Shutterstock

Standards

© 2004 Mid-continent Research for Education and Learning (McREL)
© 2007 Teachers of English to Speakers of Other Languages, Inc. (TESOL)
© 2007 Board of Regents of the University of Wisconsin System. World-Class Instructional Design and Assessment (WIDA)
© 2010 National Governors Association Center for Best Practices and Council of Chief State School Officers (CCSS)

Shell Education

5301 Oceanus Drive
Huntington Beach, CA 92649-1030
http://www.shelleducation.com
ISBN 978-1-4258-1178-5
© 2014 Shell Educational Publishing, Inc.

Table of Contents

Table of Contents *(cont.)*

A Letter to You

Dear Educator,

I want to take a moment to thank you for the inspiration that you are! As more mandates fall upon your shoulders and changes are made, I admire your drive, passion, and willingness to keep putting our students first. Every decision we make as educators should come down to one simple question: "Is this decision in the best interest of our students?" This reflects not our opinion, our philosophy, or our own agenda, but simply what is going to make the greatest impact on our students in preparing them for life and career.

As you continue to be the best you can be, I want you to take a few moments each day, look in the mirror, and smile. Come on—I know you can give me a bigger smile than that! Go for the big Cheshire Cat smile with all teeth showing. Why? Because you are sometimes your greatest cheerleader. Now, take that same smile and pass it on to colleagues, students, and parents. Attitude is catching—so let's share the one that puts smiles on others' faces! You will feel better and your day will be better.

Now, tear out this page. Tape it to a place where you will see it every... single... day. Yep! Tear it out. Tape it to the bathroom mirror, your dashboard, your desk—wherever you are sure to see it. Recite and do the following every single day—no joke.

I am appreciated!

I am amazing!

I am the difference!

From one educator to another, thank you for all you do!

—LaVonna Roth

P.S. Be sure to connect with me on social media! I would love to hear from you on these strategies and lessons.

About the Author

LaVonna Roth is an international author, speaker, and consultant. She has had the privilege of working with teachers on three continents, sharing her passion for education and how the brain learns. Her desire to keep the passion of engaging instructional delivery is evident in her ideas, presentations, workshops, and books.

LaVonna has the unique ability to teach some of the more challenging concepts in education and make them simple and doable. Her goal is for teachers to be reenergized, to experience ideas that are practical and applicable, and have a great impact on student achievement because of the effect these strategies have on how the brain learns.

As a full-time teacher, LaVonna taught students at the elementary and secondary levels in all content areas, students in ELL and gifted programs, and those in the regular classroom. Her educational degrees include a bachelor's degree in special education—teaching the hearing impaired—and two master's degrees, one in the art of teaching and another in educational leadership. In addition to other professional organizations, LaVonna serves as a board member for Florida ASCD and is an affiliate member of the Society for Neuroscience.

As an author, she has written a powerful resource notebook, *Brain-Powered Lessons to Engage All Learners*, and is a dynamic and engaging presenter.

When LaVonna isn't traveling and speaking, she relaxes by spending time with her family in the Tampa, Florida, area. She is dedicated to putting students first and supporting teachers to be the best they can be.

Acknowledgements

My family
My friends
All educators
Teacher Created Materials staff

I believe we accomplish great things when we surround ourselves with great people and take action. Thank you for all you do!

—LaVonna Roth

The Power of the Brain

"What actually changes in the brain are the strengths of the connections of neurons that are engaged together, moment by moment, in time."

—Dr. Michael Merzenich

The brain is a very powerful organ, one we do not completely understand or know everything about. Yet science reveals more and more to us each day.

As educators, we have a duty to understand how the brain learns so that we can best teach our students. If we do not have an understanding of some of the powerful tools that can help facilitate our teaching and allow us to better target the brain and learning, we lose a lot of time with our students that could be used to serve them better. Plus, the likelihood of doing as much reteaching will lessen.

This is where *Brain-Powered Lessons to Engage All Learners* comes in! The eight strategies included within the lessons are designed around how the brain learns as a foundation. In addition, they are meant to be used as a formative assessment, include higher-order thinking, increase the level of engagement in learning, and support differentiation. For detailed information on each strategy, see pages 12–19.

What Makes the Brain Learn Best

As you explore the strategies in this book, keep the following key ideas in mind.

The content being taught and learned must:

◎ be engaging

◎ be relevant

◎ make sense

◎ make meaning

◎ involve movement

◎ support memory retention

The Power of the Brain *(cont.)*

Be Engaging

In order for students to pay attention, we must engage the brain. This is the overarching theme to the rest of the elements. Too often, students are learning complacently. Just because students are staring at the teacher, with pencil in hand and taking notes, does not mean they are engaged. For example, we know that they are engaged when they answer questions or are interacting with the information independently with a teacher or another student. We don't always know when they are engaged just by looking at them. Sometimes, it's a simple question or observation of what they are doing that helps identify this. Body language can tell

> **"Even simple brain exercises such as presenting oneself with challenging intellectual environments, interacting in social situations, or getting involved in physical activities will boost the general growth of connections"** (HOPES 2010, §2).

us a lot, but do not rely on this as the only point of observation. Many teachers may have not gone into teaching to "entertain," but entertaining is one component of being engaging. As neuroscience research has revealed, it was noted as early as 1762, that the brain does change (neuroplasticity) based on experiences (Doidge 2007). It rewires itself based upon experiences and new situations, creating new neural pathways. "Even simple brain exercises such as presenting oneself with challenging intellectual environments, interacting in social situations, or getting involved in physical activities will boost the general growth of connections" (HOPES 2010, §2). This is fantastic if we are creating an environment and lessons that are positive and planned in a way that fires more neurons that increase accurate learning.

The Power of the Brain *(cont.)*

As a reflection for you, think about the following with respect to student engagement:

◎ What are the students doing during the lesson? Are they doing something with the information that shows they are into it? Are they asking questions? Are they answering?

◎ What is their body language showing? Are they slumped, or are they sitting in a more alert position? Are their eyes glazed and half-closed, or are they bright, alert, and paying attention to where their focus should be?

◎ Who is doing most of the talking and thinking? Move away from being the sage on the stage! Let the students be the stars. Share your knowledge with them in increments, but permit them to interact or explore.

◎ What could you turn over to students to have them create a way to remember the content or ask questions they have? What could be done to change up the lesson so they are interacting or standing? Yes, parts of lessons can be taught by having students stand for a minute or so. Before they sit, have them stretch or high-five a few classmates to break up the monotony.

Be Relevant

Why should the brain want to learn and remember something that has no relevance to us? If we want our students to learn information, it is important that we do what we can to make the information relevant. An easy way to achieve this is by bringing in some background knowledge that students have about the topic or making a personal connection. This does not need to take long.

As you will note, the lessons in this book start out with modeling. Modeling allows learners to have an understanding of the strategy and it also takes a moment to bring in what they know and, when possible, to make a personal connection. Consider asking students what they know about a topic and have them offer ideas. Or ask them to reflect on a piece of literature that you read or to ponder a question you have provided. For English language learners, this strategy is particularly effective when they can relate it to something of which they have a foundational concept and can make a connection to what they are learning. The language will come.

Make Sense

Is what you are teaching something that makes sense to students? Do they see the bigger picture or context? If students are making sense of what they are learning, a greater chance of it moving from working memory to long-term memory will increase. Some students can be asked if the idea makes sense and if they clearly understand. If they are able to explain it in their own words, they probably have a good grasp on metacognition and where they are in their learning. Other students may need to be coached to retell you what they just learned.

The Power of the Brain *(cont.)*

Make Meaning

Once students have had an opportunity to make sense of what they are learning, provide an opportunity for them to make meaning. This means that they have a chance to apply what was learned and actually "play" with the skills or concepts. Are they able to complete some tasks or provide questions on their own? Are they ready to take the information to higher levels that demonstrate the depth of understanding? (Refer to Webb's Depth of Knowledge for some additional insight into various levels of making meaning on pages 22–23.) For some students, simply asking a few questions related to what is being taught or having them write a reflection of what was just explained will allow you to check in on their understanding to see where they are before taking their thinking to a higher or a deeper level.

Involve Movement

This one is particularly important because of the plethora of research on movement. Dr. John Ratey wrote the book *Spark*, which documents how student achievement soars based on some changes made to students' physical education program in which students achieved their target heart-rate zone during their physical education time. Movement, particularly exercise, increases brain-derived neurotrophic factors (BDNF) that increase learning and memory (Vaynman, Ying, and Gomez-Pinilla 2004).

Knowing that getting students to achieve their target heart rate zone is not always an option, do what you can. Have students take some brain breaks that heighten their heart rate—even if for just a minute.

Movement has strong retention implications in other ways. Students can create a gesture connected to the lesson concept, or they can stand and move while they make meaning from what they learned. Movement is multisensory, thus, various regions of the brain are activated. When multiple brain pathways are stimulated, they are more likely to enter long-term potentiation from activating episodic and semantic memories.

If you come across a model lesson in this book in which not much movement is shared or you find your students have been sitting longer than you may wish (you will know because their body language will tell you—unfortunately, we should have had them moving before this point), my challenge to you is to think of what movement you can add to the lesson. It could involve a gesture, a manipulative, or physically getting up and moving. If you are concerned about them calming back down, set your expectations and stick to them. Keep in mind that often when students "go crazy" when permitted to move, it's probably because they *finally* get to move. Try simple techniques to bring students back into focus. "Part of the process of assisting children in developing necessary skills is getting to the root of why they behave as they do" (Harris and Goldberg 2012, xiv).

The Power of the Brain *(cont.)*

Support Memory Retention

If we want our students to retain what we teach them, then it is important that we keep in mind what causes our brains to retain that information.

Key Elements to Memory Retention	Why
Emotions	We can create an episodic memory when we connect emotions to our learning.
Repetition	Repetition increases memory as long as there is engagement involved. Worksheets and drill and kill do not serve long-term memory well.
Patterns/Organization	When our brains take in messages, they begin to file the information by organizing it into categories.
Personal connection	Linking learning to one's self is a powerful brain tool for memory. This, too, can be tied to emotion, making an even stronger connection.
Linking new and prior knowledge	Taking in new information automatically results in connecting past knowledge to what is new.

(Roth 2012)

As you explore the strategies and lessons throughout this book, note how many of them incorporate the keys to memory retention and what engages our students' brains. As you begin to explore the use of these strategies on your own, be sure to keep the framework of those important components.

The bottom line—explore, have fun, and ask your students how they feel about lessons taught. They will tell you if they found the lesson interesting, engaging, and relevant. So get in there, dig in, and have some fun with your students while trying out these strategies and lessons!

Sort It
Strategy Overview

As our brains take in information, we immediately connect it to something known and begin filing it accordingly (Willis 2008). Each lobe of the brain takes responsibility for different information that is transferred across regions by a massive neural system that would put social networks out of business. The corpus callosum, connecting both hemispheres, assists in the networking, allowing the two hemispheres to interact and help each other out (Vermillion 2010). Sousa (2006) explains that the brain evaluates new stimuli for clues to help connect incoming information with stored patterns, categories of data, or past experiences, thereby extending existing patterns with the new input. Once the sensory input reaches the hippocampus, it is ready to fuse into memory (Eldridge et al. 2010). This fusion, however, can only occur if the prior knowledge in stored memory is first activated and sent to the hippocampus to connect with the new information.

Strategy Insight

In the *Sort It* strategy, students look for patterns, trends, or common themes as they sort through information and move around at the same time. Movement increases oxygen levels in the brain, which improves attention and leads to engagement. We are in a better position to learn when we move (Sousa 2006). In addition, the brain thrives on making predictions. Students predict where they think they fit and why. This is an important step in the learning process. Being wrong and being right helps our brain lock in on the learning. Either we are right and the brain celebrates with a burst of dopamine (pleasure) or we correct our thinking and the brain takes note of the correction because it wants to be right. This strategy allows students to make predictions about the topic of study and then explain their thinking. Students will have the opportunity to tap into their thinking, which provides the teacher an insight into where to make a correction or to celebrate their connection.

Throughout this process, students interact with the content while taking their thinking to a higher level. They physically move while looking at other students' cards and determine where they belong. During this process, they have already begun to predict as to what category they belong, and as they walk around, they confirm or shift their thinking based on what they see. Since there is the possibility of more than one answer, students can analyze and rearrange their original thoughts to justify the choices they make.

Teacher Notes

◎ Differentiate by giving easier words or concepts to students who are struggling. **Note:** We often underestimate the ability of a student. Let them struggle some so they learn, but not so much that they become frustrated.

◎ During the mingle part of the strategy, tell students to work with various students and not the same people each time.

It Takes Two
Strategy Overview

In this strategy, students compare and contrast two topics (e.g., stories, historical figures, types of clouds and shapes) using a T-chart and sticky notes. The goal is for students to analyze each topic and create a chart that represents their thinking. Thereafter, another group of students will evaluate whether it agrees with the original group's thoughts or if not, if it is going to propose another way to think about the topic. The goal is for students to be able to think at a higher level by justifying either what each sticky note says and where each one is placed or if it qualifies to be on the T-chart at all.

Strategy Insight

Organization and thinking critically are key components in this strategy. Since we organize ideas in our brains systematically and create a neural pathway as more modalities are used, students increase their learning by seeing the information, sorting through what is important, organizing the facts by what is similar and what is different, and adding another level of value through student interaction (Van Tassell 2004). Each of these components plays an integral part in student engagement and retention (Covington 2000). It is another way for students to work with content at a level that is minds-on and hands-on.

Using sticky notes during this activity is important (as opposed to recording the similarities and differences on a sheet) because students' thinking will shift as they discuss and learn more. The sticky notes allow the graphic organizer to become manipulative, and it is a new way for them to see if they agree or disagree with their classmates and adjust accordingly.

Teacher Notes

◎ It is imperative that teachers observe during all stages of the lesson. This provides the feedback we need to determine the next direction of instruction. In addition, it allows an opportunity to guide students in their thinking, as some may struggle with concepts at a higher level. **Note:** Do not guide too much. A large part of learning is struggling through the process with a small amount of frustration but not so much that students give up.

◎ During discussions, students will likely discover that there can be more than one answer. That is where collaboration and cooperation pay off.

◎ For younger students, reconvene as a whole group and model the evaluation steps, using one group's chart.

ABC Professors
Strategy Overview

This strategy is best used after students have studied a topic. They become "professors" or "experts" because they have the knowledge base that is necessary to complete a task about the topic.

After students are taught what they need to know, have them begin thinking about the topic. Portions of the strategy are modeled. Then students, with guidance, brainstorm words or phrases about their topic that begin with each letter of the alphabet. The goal is to have a word or phrase for each letter of the alphabet filled in on their *ABC Professor Notes* activity sheet (page 72). This strategy is motivating and can ease the challenging task of asking more inquisitive questions.

Strategy Insight

Although this strategy is meant as a review, it could be used as a formative preassessment to see what students know before a topic is introduced and then used again to see the growth that occurred after teaching the topic. Once students are comfortable with the strategy, they can be given the opportunity to choose their own topic (McCombs 1997).

This strategy can be used as a "sneak peek" to find out what students know, but teachers should watch for the level of frustration. When too much frustration occurs, the stress blockers begin to hinder thinking, and learning declines (Medina 2008). Teachers should challenge students so that their brains seek the pleasure of the intrinsic rewards of learning. According to Csikszentmihalyi (1996), teachers need to keep students in the "flow," a level of challenge that is not too high or low and one that keeps them motivated and engaged, as well.

During the Evaluate/Create component of the strategy, students are challenged to ask questions in alphabetical order and provide a response to the questions their partners ask. Students do not necessarily need to answer the questions. This strategy is to get them thinking and wondering, becoming curious enough to seek answers or speculate about possible answers.

Teacher Notes

◎ Not every box needs to be filled when completing the *ABC Professor Notes* activity sheet. Instead of limiting the number of letters or excluding certain letters, make it a challenge for certain identified students to see how many quality words or phrases they can think of. If it becomes apparent that they have reached a high level of frustration, then ask them which boxes they would like to reasonably eliminate.

◎ If using this as a priming activity, have students record their responses so that they can assess what they used to think, what they now think, and the depth of learning that occurred as they reflect back.

Kinesthetic Word Webs
Strategy Overview

Movement is crucial to learning. We must move because the "sit-and-get" method is overused and not as effective as when we have the chance to increase our oxygen intake and shift the activity. Although there is no exact science as to the number of minutes that elapse before we should move or change direction, no more than 20 minutes is an adequate amount of time for learning to occur before we do something with what was learned (Schenck 2005). Our working memory can only hold so much information before it becomes fatigued or bored (Sousa 2006). Thus, implementing the suggested 20-minute time frame into teaching should help teachers to remember the importance of chunking material and allowing time for the brain to process material being learned.

We know what a web is on paper, but what is a *Kinesthetic Word Web*? It is a strategy that gets students up and moving with the content of the lessons. Picture a word web on paper. Now, turn the outer ovals on the word web into students and imagine their arms touching the person's shoulder in the center oval. That is a Kinesthetic Word Web.

Strategy Insight

The *Kinesthetic Word Webs* strategy is designed to take a paper-and-pencil activity and add movement and challenge to raise the level of engagement. As Wolfe and Brandt (1998) stated, "The brain likes a challenge!" It seeks patterns. Patterns are required during this strategy in order to be successful.

Teacher Notes

◎ Be sure every student has a card. Do not worry about every student fitting into a word web. If a student cannot be a part of a *Kinesthetic Word Web* because his or her word has already appeared in the web or because there was not an exact number of students for each set, they can explain where they would go and why.

◎ **Note:** Some students do not like to be touched, so knowing students and their backgrounds is very important. As an alternative, they can each place a fist on a hip and connect elbow to elbow; they can extend a leg and touch foot to foot; or you can provide 15 inches of string to each student, with the center student holding one end of all the strings.

Matchmaker
Strategy Overview

The importance of movement and having students get up out of their seats cannot be emphasized enough. Thus, here is another strategy that allows our students to do so. *Matchmaker* also provides students an opportunity to get repeated practice in an environment in which the repetition is guided and correct. This means that when students practice repeatedly, the likelihood of recall increases. A key factor here is that it must be correct practice. When students do this activity with one another, they are getting a chance to see repeated practice with automatic feedback provided about whether they are correct or not.

Strategy Insight

Every student is given an address label to wear. Each label is a vocabulary word, a concept, a formula, etc. On the index cards are the matching definitions, illustrations, examples, synonyms, etc.

Students wear the address labels and stand in a circle with the index cards on the floor in the middle. Students hold hands and bend down to pick up an index card with their connected hands. Without letting go, they have to get the card they picked up to the correct person, according to his or her address label. This strategy can be repeated as many times as you wish to help students practice.

Teacher Notes

◎ An alternative to this is for students to not hold hands when they pick up a card. However, energy and engagement increase with the added challenge of holding hands and not letting go.

◎ Be sure to listen in and encourage students to discuss disagreements or to have them respond to a reason why a particular card goes with another card.

Just Say It
Strategy Overview

Working together and hearing thoughts and language are beneficial to all learners, but these things can be especially beneficial to English language learners. *Just Say It* permits students not only to use what they have read, written, or heard but to have a chance to use listening skills for the content, as well. A challenge layer to this strategy is having students hold back on a response for a period of time. This allows the one student to say what he or she needs to say before the partner inflicts his or her opinion or factual information upon him or her. It teaches the skill of patience, listening, and being open to others' thoughts at the same time.

Strategy Insight

Students are to respond to their partners, providing feedback and information on a given topic (e.g., a writing prompt, thoughts, an idea). Have students sit facing their partners (sitting at desks is preferable). Identify Partner *A* as the person closest to the front of the room and Partner *B* as the person closest to the back of room. Have Partner *A* start. Partner *A* shares his or her thinking with Partner *B* as partner *B* only listens for 30 seconds. After 30 seconds, Partner *B* responds to Partner *A*. They then switch roles—Partner *B* shares while *A* listens. Then *A* provides insight or feedback. Students should record (during or at the end), what their partners say for further consideration and use that to write about the topic.

Teacher Notes

◎ You may wish to shorten or lengthen the time each partner has, depending upon the topic and age.

◎ Using a timer, a train whistle, or a bell is a great way to help partners know when to switch, since conversations may get lively or partners may tune out other nearby sounds.

Show It with Dough!
Strategy Overview

Our brains recall pictures quite well. This phenomenon is called the *Pictorial Superiority Effect* (PSE) (Medina 2008). Simply put, the brain grasps pictures and can recognize and recall a picture with far less effort than it takes to recall text.

Through the use of dough sculptures, students think about a concept and make a three-dimensional representation, often moving from abstract to concrete ideas. This is a higher-level skill since it requires extended thinking to represent something in a new way (Bloom 1956).

Strategy Insight

Many concepts we teach are quite abstract, particularly as students progress in grade levels. This strategy often requires students to visualize the concept on a concrete level rather than an abstract level. Thus, this strategy is at a higher level because students are being asked to demonstrate their learning in a new way. Additionally, we are asking students to connect their visual representations to what they already know; therefore, we also incorporate activating prior knowledge and experiences, which in turn ties in to something personal. This strategy can also impact other content areas and allows students the opportunity to use their creativity in an expressive way.

Teacher Notes

◎ Walk around as students create their sculptures and ask them to think about what they are making, and why. Consider doing this very quietly so others do not hear what they are creating, or use written communication.

◎ Place student sculptures on cardboard so they are easy to move or display.

◎ After students add more detail to their sculptures and write their stories, display them where others can enjoy them.

Reverse, Reverse!
Strategy Overview

Reverse, Reverse! is meant to be a challenging strategy. When students are under stress, there will often be not only a chemical but a physical change in the brain. Students must learn the skills to deal with stress, but in a safe and friendly environment. In this strategy, students will practice the speed and fluency of facts, but they will do so under pressure—a pressure that you can adjust or increase, depending upon the topic and age level of your students.

Strategy Insight

Students sit or stand in a circle. They are given a topic to brainstorm what they know about that topic. One student begins by sharing a fact about the topic. Going clockwise, the next student must quickly say another fact related to the one just stated. If the student pauses more than five seconds or states an incorrect fact, the student that just finished must pick up the next fact (reversing the direction of participation). One student sits out to judge the facts and make sure rules are followed. Continue until participation stalls. For example, a math activity using this strategy can include counting by threes. The first student says, "3;" the next student says, "6;" the next says, "9." If the following student says, "13," the rotation reverses to the previous student, who must say, "Reverse" and must also say the correct answer, "12." The responses are now going counterclockwise. An example of using this strategy in social studies can include the three branches of government. The first student might say, "Legislative branch," the second says, "Makes the laws;" the third student says, "Congress;" and the fourth says, "Checks and balances." The judge (student sitting out) can halt the flow to ask how the response relates to a previously said fact. If justified, the round continues. *Reverse, Reverse!* continues until a predetermined amount of clock time or number of times around the circle has been met.

Teacher Notes

◎ It is important to set the stage for students to feel safe when using this strategy. You may wish to take out the reverse portion at first and work on just the speed. Add the extra layer of difficulty for novelty and time-pressured practice.

◎ For younger students, you may choose to not have the next student say, "Reverse," but instead state the correct fact.

How to Use This Book

Lesson Overview

The following lesson components are in each lesson and establish the flow and success of the lessons.

Icons state the brain-powered strategy and one of the four content areas addressed in the book: language arts, mathematics, science, or social studies.

Each lesson revolves around one of the eight **brain-powered strategies** in this book. Be sure to review the description of each strategy found on pages 12–19.

Vocabulary that will be addressed in the lesson is called out in case extra support is needed.

The **procedures** provide step-by-step instructions on how to implement the lessons successfully.

The **standard** indicates the objective for the lesson.

A **materials** list identifies the components of the lesson.

Many lessons contain a **preparation note** that indicates action needed prior to implementing the lessons. Be sure to review these notes to ensure a successful delivery of the lesson.

The **model** section of the lesson provides teachers the opportunity to model what is expected of students and what needs to be accomplished throughout the lesson.

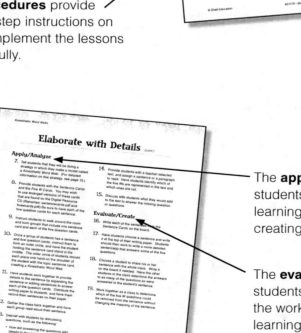

The **apply/analyze** section of the lesson provides students with the opportunity to apply what they are learning as they analyze the content and work toward creating a personal connection.

The **evaluate/create** section of the lesson provides students with the opportunity to think critically about the work of others and then to take ownership of their learning by designing the content in a way that makes sense to them.

How to Use This Book *(cont.)*

Lesson Overview *(cont.)*

Some lessons require **activity cards** to be used. You may wish to laminate the activity cards for added durability. Be sure to read the preparation note in each lesson to prepare the activity cards, when applicable.

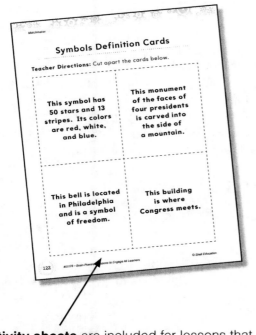

Activity sheets are included for lessons that require them. They are to be used either in groups, individually, or just by the teacher. If students are working in groups, encourage them to create a group name to label the activity sheet.

All of the activity sheets and additional teacher resources can be found on the **Digital Resource CD**.

How to Use This Book *(cont.)*

Implementing Higher-Order Thinking in the Lessons

What Is Higher-Order Thinking?

Higher-order thinking occurs on a different level than memorizing facts or telling something back to someone exactly the way it was told (Thomas and Thorne 2009). As educators, it is important to be aware of the level of thinking that students are asked to do. If teachers record the number of questions they ask students on a recall or restate level as well as how many were asked at a higher level, they may be surprised at the imbalance. How do they expect students to think at a higher level if they are not challenged with higher-order questions and problems? Students should be given questions and assignments that require higher-order thinking.

Higher-order thinking also involves critical thinking. If teachers want students to remember facts and think critically, they need to have them be engaged and working with the content at a higher level so that it creates understanding and depth. In addition, higher-order thinking and critical thinking are imperative to 21st century skills. Employers want workers who can problem-solve and work cooperatively to find multiple solutions. The lessons in this resource gradually place more ownership of the learning process in the hands of students as they simultaneously move through higher-order thinking.

Bloom's Taxonomy and Webb's Depth of Knowledge

Throughout the history of education, structures were created to guide teachers in ways to evoke higher-order thinking. Two of the more popular structures are Bloom's Taxonomy and Webb's Depth of Knowledge (DOK).

Benjamin Bloom developed Bloom's Taxonomy as a way to classify educational learning objectives in a hierarchy. In 2001, Lorin Anderson, a former student of Bloom's, worked with some teachers to revise Bloom's original taxonomy by changing the terminology into verbs and switching the top two levels so that *create* (synthesis) is at the top and *evaluate* (evaluation) is just below (Overbaugh and Schultz n.d.).

Norman Webb created Depth of Knowledge in 1997 in order to assist with aligning the depth and complexity of a standard with its assessment. This structure focuses on how the verb is used in the context of what is asked of the student (Webb 2005). DOK correlates with Backwards Planning (Wiggins and McTighe 2005) in that the standards are addressed first and then an assessment that targets the standards is developed or selected.

How to Use This Book *(cont.)*

It is important that teachers instruct students at cognitive levels that meet their needs while challenging them, as well. Whether students are below level, on level, or above level, teachers should use the tools necessary to help them succeed. Using Webb's DOK gives us the tools to look at the end result and tie complexity to the assessment. Bloom's Taxonomy helps to guide depth of assignments and questions. Where the two meet is with the word complexity. Complexity is rigor. Complexity is the changing of levels within Bloom's, and DOK is the amount of depth of thinking that must occur. We want rigor, and thus we want complexity in our teachings.

Bloom's Taxonomy	Webb's Depth of Knowledge
Knowledge/Remembering The recall of specifics and universals, involving little more than bringing to mind the appropriate material.	**Recall** The recall of a fact, information, or procedure (e.g., What are three critical-skill cues for the overhand throw?).
Comprehension/Understanding The ability to process knowledge on a low level such that the knowledge can be reproduced or communicated without a verbatim repetition.	**Skill/Concept** The use of information, conceptual knowledge, procedures, two or more steps, etc.
Application/Applying The ability to use information in another familiar situation.	**Strategy Thinking** Requires reasoning, developing a plan, or sequence of steps; has some complexity; more than one possible answer.
Analysis/Analyzing The ability to break information into parts to explore understandings and relationships.	**Extended Thinking** Requires an investigation as well as time to think and process multiple conditions of the problem or task.
Synthesis and Evaluation/Evaluating and Creating Putting together elements and parts to form a whole and then making value judgements about the method.	

Adapted from Wyoming School Health and Physical Education (2001)

Correlation to the Standards

Shell Education is committed to producing educational materials that are research and standards based. In this effort, we have correlated all of our products to the academic standards of all 50 states, the District of Columbia, the Department of Defense Dependents Schools, and all Canadian provinces.

How to Find Standards Correlations

To print a customized correlation report of this product for your state, visit our website at http://www.shelleducation.com and follow the on-screen directions. If you require assistance in printing correlation reports, please contact our Customer Service department at 1-877-777-3450.

Purpose and Intent of Standards

Legislation mandates that all states adopt academic standards that identify the skills students will learn in kindergarten through grade twelve. Many states also have standards for Pre–K. This same legislation sets requirements to ensure the standards are detailed and comprehensive.

Standards are designed to focus instruction and guide adoption of curricula. Standards are statements that describe the criteria necessary for students to meet specific academic goals. They define the knowledge, skills, and content students should acquire at each level. Standards are also used to develop standardized tests to evaluate students' academic progress. Teachers are required to demonstrate how their lessons meet state standards. State standards are used in the development of all of our products, so educators can be assured they meet the academic requirements of each state.

Common Core State Standards

Many lessons in this book are aligned to the Common Core State Standards (CCSS). The standards support the objectives presented throughout the lessons and are provided on the Digital Resource CD (filename: standards.pdf).

TESOL and WIDA Standards

The lessons in this book promote English language development for English language learners. The standards listed on the Digital Resource CD (filename: standards.pdf) support the language objectives presented throughout the lessons.

Standards Chart

Common Core State Standard	Lesson(s)
Reading 1.5—With guidance and support from adults, demonstrate understanding of word relationships and nuances in word meanings	What Does It Mean? p. 114
Reading: Foundational Skills.1.2.a—Distinguish long from short vowel sounds in spoken single-syllable words	Vowel Sort p. 29
Reading: Informational Text.1.2—Identify the main topic and retell key details of a text	There Is Support p. 81
Reading: Literature.1.3—Describe characters, settings, and major events in a story, using key details	Characters: Same and Different p. 62
Reading: Literature.1.9—Compare and contrast the adventures and experiences of characters in stories	Character Connections p. 125
Language.1.1.c—Use singular and plural nouns with matching verbs in basic sentences	Nouns and Verbs p. 70
Writing.1.1—Write opinion pieces in which they introduce the topic or name the book they are writing about, state an opinion, supply a reason for the opinion, and provide some sense of closure	In My Opinion p. 65
Writing.1.2—Write informative/explanatory texts in which they name a topic, supply some facts about the topic, and provide some sense of closure	Expanding Details p. 128
Writing.1.3—Write narratives in which they recount two or more appropriately sequenced events, include some details regarding what happened, use temporal words to signal event order, and provide some sense of closure	Narrative Writing p. 136
Writing.1.5—With guidance and support from adults, focus on a topic, respond to questions and suggestions from peers, and add details to strengthen writing as needed	Elaborate with Details p. 89
Math.1.NBT—Count to 120, starting at any number less than 120	Counting p. 145

Standards Chart (cont.)

Common Core State Standard	Lesson(s)
Math.1.OA.2—Solve word problems that call for addition of three whole numbers whose sum is less than or equal to 20, e.g., by using objects, drawings, and equations with a symbol for the unknown number to represent the problem	Adding Three Numbers p. 130
Math.1.OA.3—Apply properties of operations as strategies to add	Number Representations p. 97
Math.1.MD.1—Order three objects by length; compare the lengths of two objects indirectly by using a third object	Is Bigger Better? p. 68
Math.1.G.1—Distinguish between defining attributes versus non-defining attributes; build and draw shapes to possess defining attributes	Attributes of Shapes p. 44

McREL Standard	Lesson(s)
Science 1.1—Knows that short-term weather conditions can change daily and weather patterns change over the seasons	Wonderful Weather p. 73
Science 5.2—Knows that plants and animals have features that help them live in different environments	Plant Parts p. 140; Animal Types p. 148
Science 8.1—Knows that different objects are made of many different types of materials and have many different observable properties	Sink or Float? p. 58
Science 12.1—Knows that learning can come from careful observation and simple experiments	What Do You Observe? p. 133
History 1.1—Knows that goods are objects that can satisfy people's wants, and services are activities that can satisfy people's wants	Goods and Services p. 106
History 2.1—Understands changes in community over time	Life Long Ago p. 77
History 4.8—Knows the history of American symbols	It Represents the U.S. p. 117
History 4.9—Knows why important buildings, statues, and monuments are associated with state and national history	It Represents the U.S. p. 117

Standards Chart *(cont.)*

McREL Standard	Lesson(s)
Geography 1.0—Understands the characteristics and uses of maps, globes, and other geographic tools and technologies	Map Maker p. 151
Geography 4.2—Knows that places can be defined in terms of their predominant human and physical characteristics	Map It Out p. 143

TESOL and WIDA Standard	Lesson(s)
English language learners **communicate** for **social, intercultural,** and **instructional** purposes within the school setting	All Lessons
English language learners **communicate** information, ideas, and concepts necessary for academic success in the area of **language arts**	All Lessons

Content Area Correlations Chart

Content Area	Lessons
Reading	Vowel Sort p. 29; Characters: Same and Different p. 62; Nouns and Verbs p. 70; There Is Support p. 81; What Does It Mean? p. 114; Character Connections p. 125
Writing	In My Opinion p. 65; Elaborate with Details p. 89; Expanding Details p. 128; Narrative Writing p. 136
Math	Attributes of Shapes p. 44; Is Bigger Better? p. 68; Number Representations p. 97; Adding Three Numbers p. 130; Counting p. 145
Social Studies	Life Long Ago p. 77; Goods and Services p. 106; It Represents the U.S. p. 117; Map It Out p. 143; Map Maker p. 151
Science	Sink or Float? p. 58; Wonderful Weather p. 73; What Do You Observe? p. 133; Plant Parts p. 140; Animal Types p. 148

Vowel Sort

Brain-Powered Strategy	Standard
Sort It	Distinguish long from short vowel sounds in spoken single-syllable words

Vocabulary Words	**Materials**
• long vowel • short vowel • syllable	• *Vowel Picture Cards* (pages 31–42) • *Short and Long Word Cards* (page 43) • chart paper • marker • music

Preparation Note: Prior to the lesson, cut apart the *Vowel Picture Cards* (pages 31–42) and the *Short and Long Word Cards* (page 43). Have enough available so that each student can have a card. You may have more than one copy of the same word. Additionally, create a two-column chart. Label one side *Short Vowel*s and the other side *Long Vowels*.

Procedures

Model

1. Review short vowel and long vowel sounds with students, as needed.

2. Say the word *can*, one sound at a time, emphasizing the vowel sound. Record the word (or draw a quick picture) on the short vowel side of the chart.

3. Repeat Step 2 with the word *cane* and record it on the long vowel side of the chart.

4. Say each of the following words, one sound at a time, emphasizing the vowel sound: *pet, mop, peach, cub,* and *kite*. Have students help identify if each word has a long or short vowel sound, and record the word in the correct column.

Apply/Analyze

5. Distribute the *Vowel Picture Cards* to students, one card per student. Have students stand behind their chairs and name the pictures on the cards they were given.

6. Tell students that they will be using a strategy called *Sort It*. (For detailed information on this strategy, see page 12.) Explain to students that they have words that have either long vowel or short vowel sounds and that they must sort themselves according to the vowel sounds.

7. Play music as students mingle around the room. Once students have sorted themselves, have them share with each other why they belong together.

Vowel Sort *(cont.)*

8. Collect the cards and play again, but this time, mix in the *Short and Long Word Cards*. Have students sort themselves by finding the long and short vowel words that have the same vowel sounds. For example, students with short *a* (*mad*) and long *a* (*maid*) would stand together.

Evaluate/Create

9. Have students return to their desks.

10. Choose either deck of cards or mix the two decks of cards together and redistribute them to students.

11. Have students form pairs. Provide time for students to identify whether their words have short vowels or long vowels.

12. Ask the pairs to decide if they belong together or not and why. For example, students could say that they both have short vowels or that they both have the same vowel letter, even if one has a long vowel and one has a short vowel, or that they do not belong together because one has a short vowel sound and one has a long vowel sound and the vowel is not the same letter. Students should be able to justify their reasoning.

13. Have several pairs of students share aloud their words and whether it is a short or long vowel. Then, have the pair share aloud why they do or do not belong together.

Vowel Picture Cards

Teacher Directions: Cut apart the cards below.

mad

maid

#51178—*Brain-Powered Lessons to Engage All Learners*

Vowel Picture Cards *(cont.)*

bed

bee

Vowel Picture Cards *(cont.)*

kit

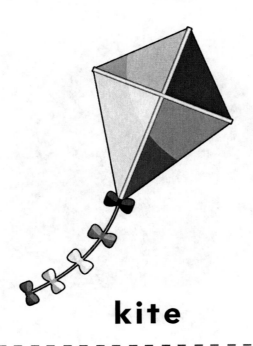

kite

Vowel Picture Cards *(cont.)*

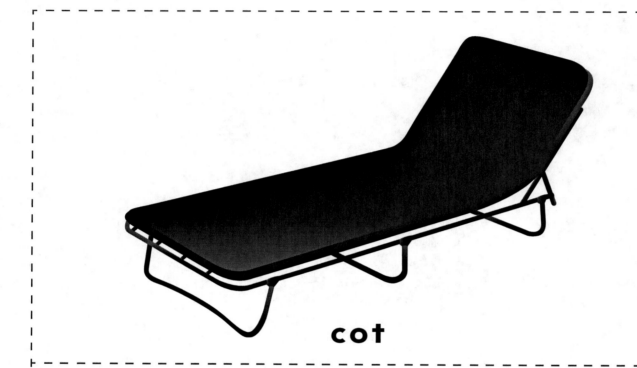

cot

coat

Vowel Picture Cards (cont.)

man

mane

Vowel Picture Cards (cont.)

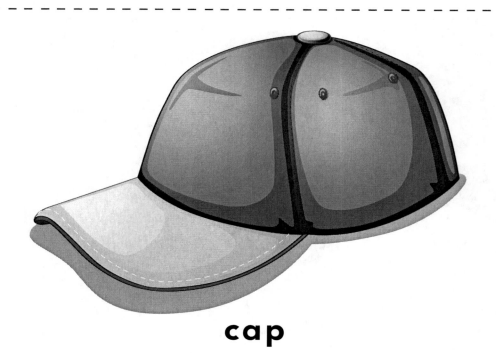

cap

cape

Vowel Picture Cards *(cont.)*

cub

cube

Vowel Picture Cards *(cont.)*

red

read

Vowel Picture Cards *(cont.)*

knot

Dear Mom,

Thank you for a great birthday.

Love,
Tom

note

#51178—Brain-Powered Lessons to Engage All Learners

Vowel Picture Cards (cont.)

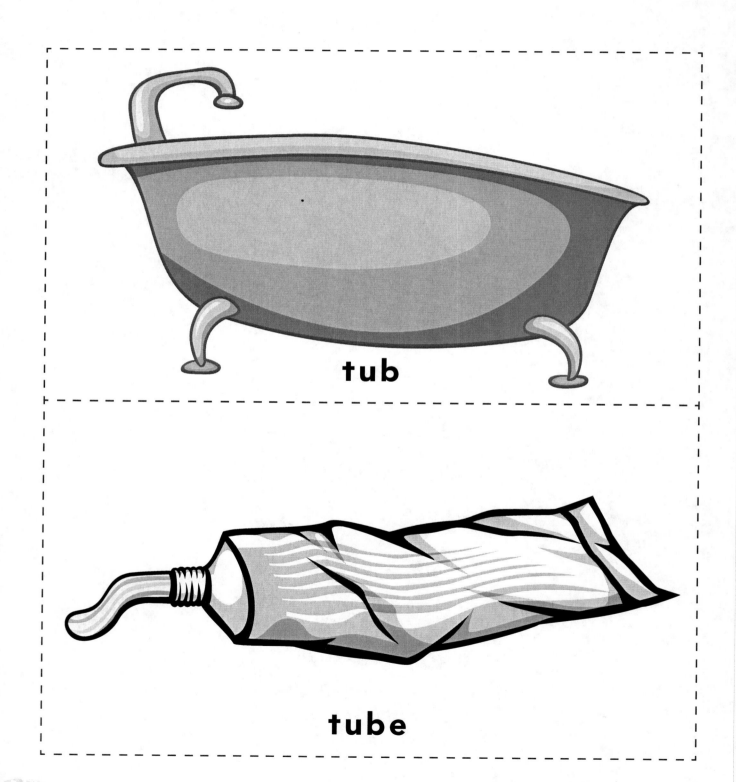

tub

tube

Vowel Picture Cards *(cont.)*

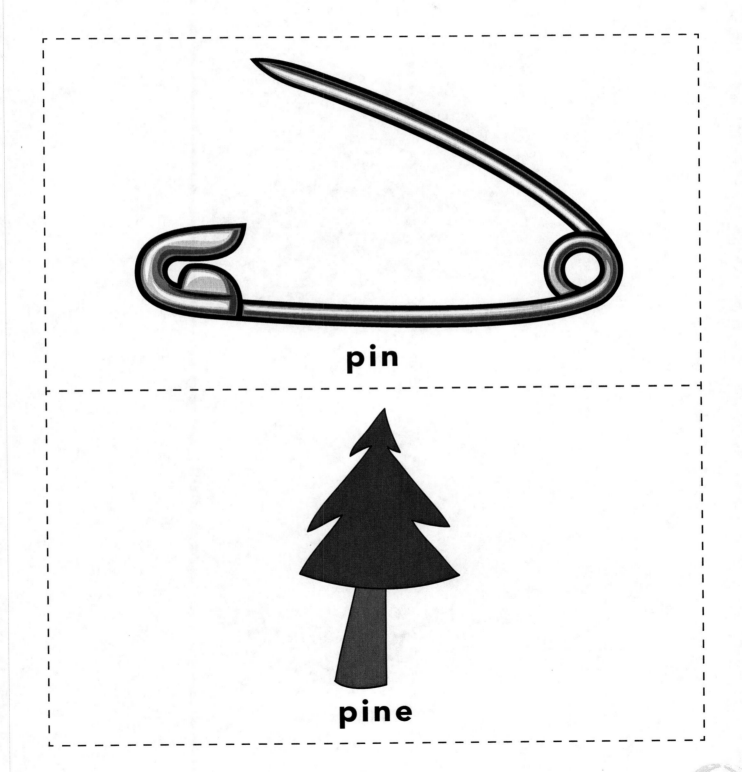

pin

pine

Vowel Picture Cards (cont.)

tap

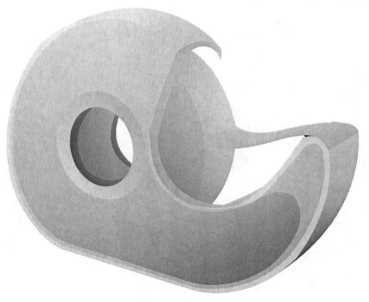

tape

 #51178—*Brain-Powered Lessons to Engage All Learners*

Short and Long Word Cards

Teacher Directions: Cut apart the cards below.

Short Vowel	**Long Vowel**
Short Vowel	**Long Vowel**
Short Vowel	**Long Vowel**

Attributes of Shapes

Brain-Powered Strategy	Standard
Sort It	Distinguish between defining attributes versus non-defining attributes; build and draw shapes to possess defining attributes

Vocabulary Words

- attribute
- curved
- side
- straight
- vertex

Materials

- *Shape Cards* (pages 46–57)
- shape book (e.g., *The Greedy Triangle* by Marilyn Burns)
- attribute or pattern blocks
- music
- drawing paper
- crayons or markers

Preparation Note: Prior to the lesson, cut apart the *Shape Cards* (pages 46–57). Have enough available so each student can have a card. You may have more than one copy of the same card.

Procedures

Model

1. Read aloud portions of the chosen shape book to students in order to activate prior knowledge.

2. Draw the following shapes on the board: circle, square, triangle, and rectangle.

3. Distribute a square block to each student. Explain that a line segment is a part of a figure known as a *side*. Ask students to trace their finger along the side of the shape.

4. Point to the corners of the square. Explain that a *vertex* is where two line segments meet to create a point. Have students practice identifying the vertices on their squares, and then count the number of sides and number of vertices.

5. Let students know that what they just learned are attributes of a square.

6. Repeat Steps 3 and 4 with the remaining shapes. Differentiate between curved and straight sides. If desired, ask questions such as the following:

   - *How many vertices does a _____ have?*
   - *If the _____ is turned, is it still a _____?*

Attributes of Shapes *(cont.)*

Apply/Analyze

7. Distribute the *Shape Cards* to students, one card per student. Have students stand behind their chairs and look at the shapes on the cards they were given.

8. Tell students that they will be doing a strategy called *Sort It*. (For detailed information on this strategy, see page 12.) Explain to students that they must sort themselves according to the attributes of their shapes.

9. Play music as students mingle around the room. Once students have sorted themselves, have them share with one another why they belong together.

10. Collect, shuffle, and redistribute the cards and have students play again.

Evaluate/Create

11. Provide each student with a variety of pattern blocks. Have students independently create composite shapes by taking two squares to make a rectangle. Ask students to count the number of sides and vertices on the newly created shape.

12. Distribute drawing paper to students. Allow students to explore the creation of other new shapes. They should draw their composite shapes showing the shapes they used. Encourage them to label their illustrations with vocabulary words.

13. Have students share and discuss their creations with partners. Instruct them to use at least three vocabulary words during their discussion.

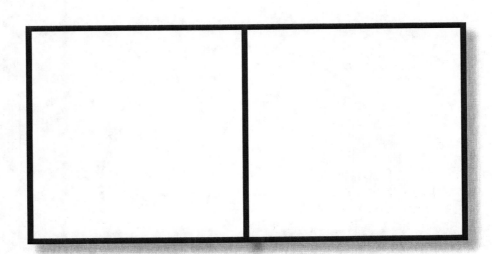

Shape Cards

Teacher Directions: Cut apart the cards below.

Shape Cards *(cont.)*

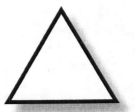

Shape Cards (cont.)

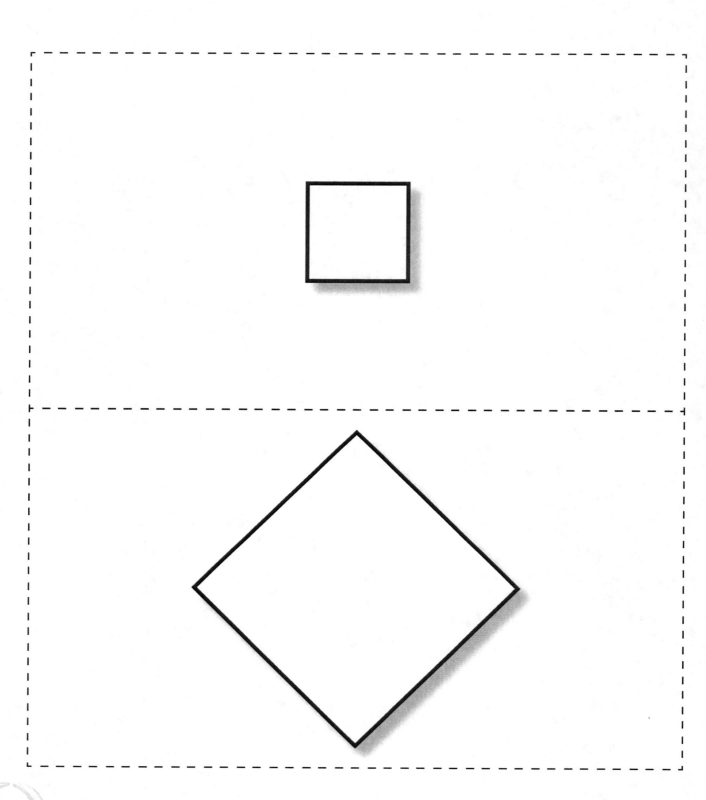

Shape Cards *(cont.)*

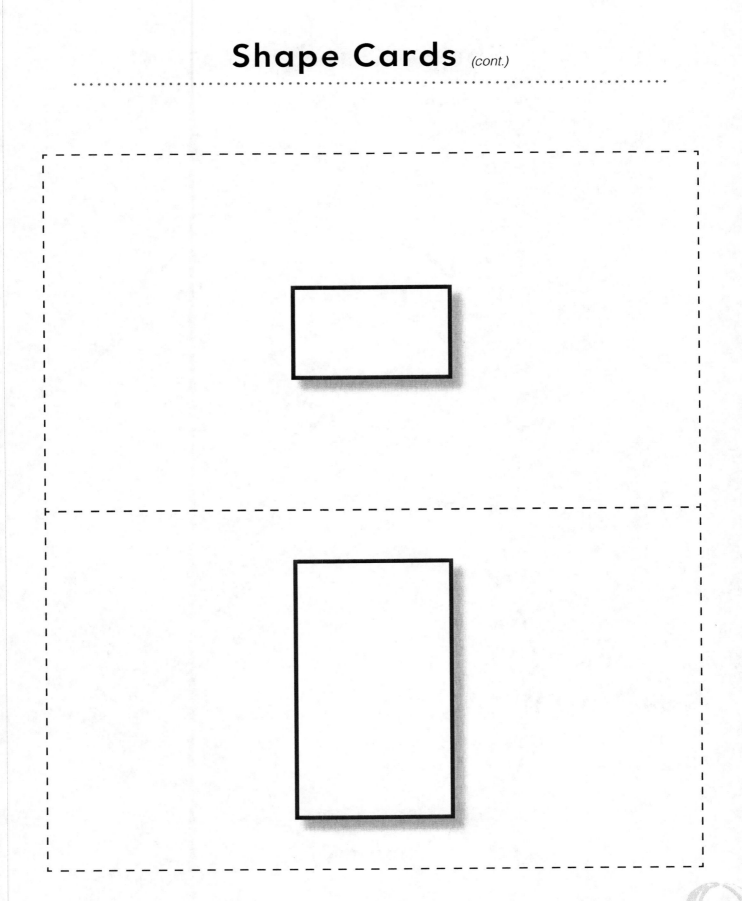

Shape Cards *(cont.)*

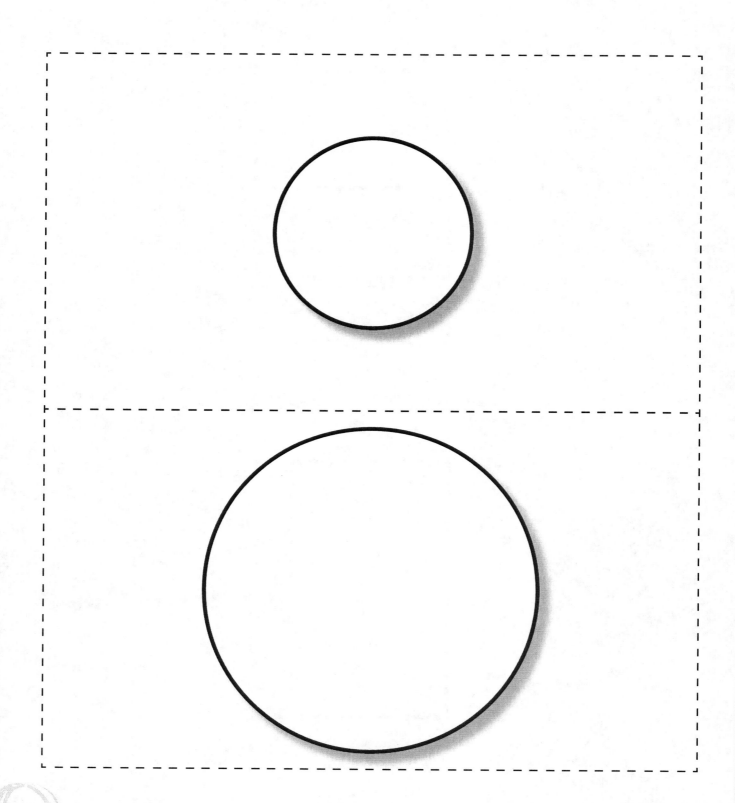

Shape Cards *(cont.)*

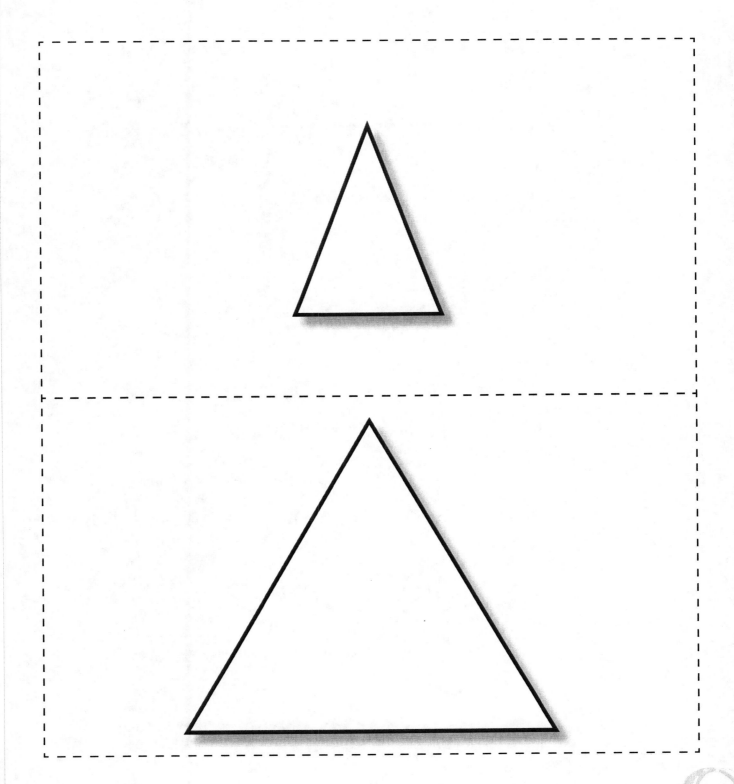

Shape Cards *(cont.)*

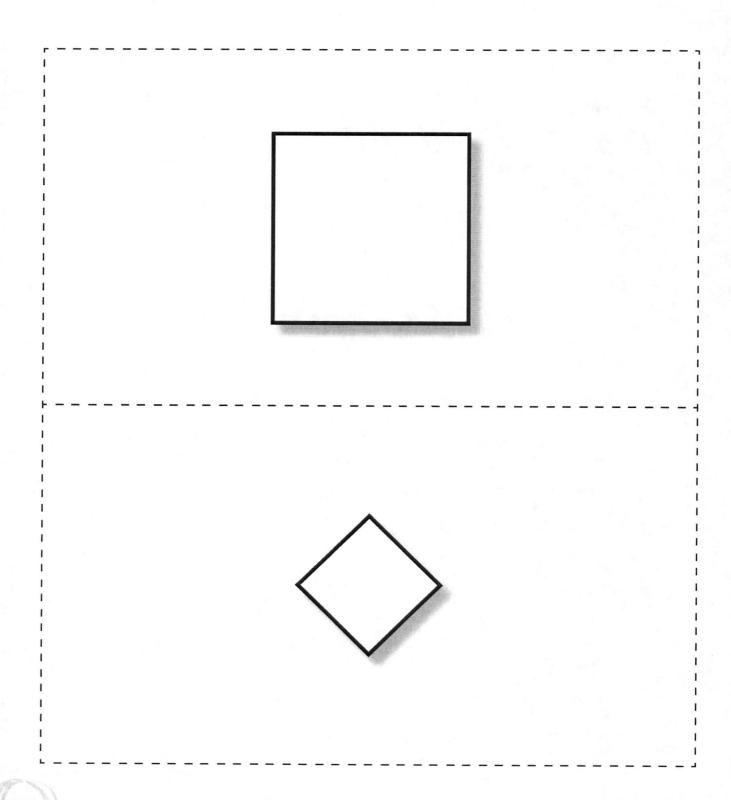

Shape Cards *(cont.)*

#51178—Brain-Powered Lessons to Engage All Learners

Shape Cards *(cont.)*

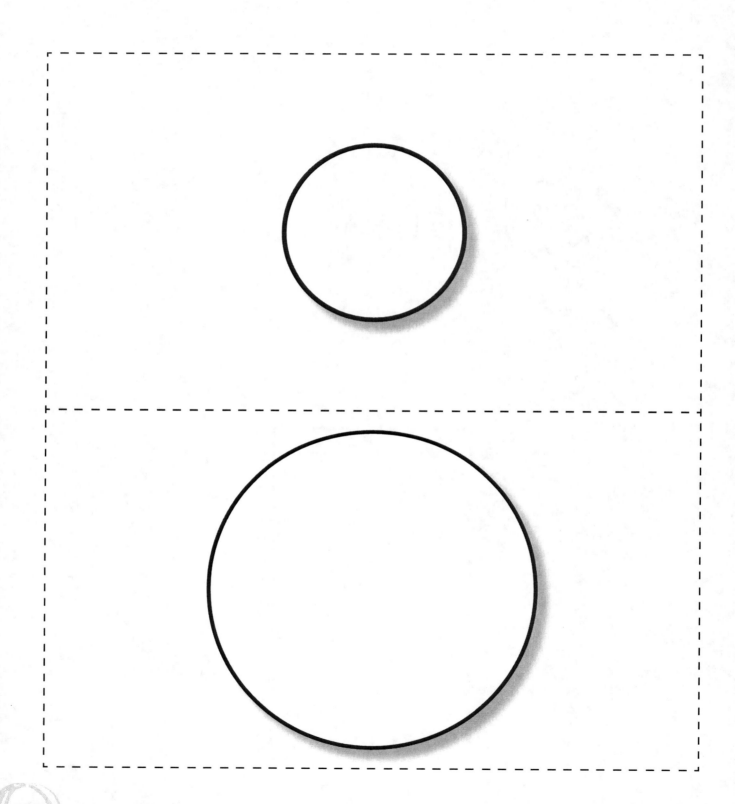

Shape Cards *(cont.)*

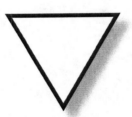

Shape Cards (cont.)

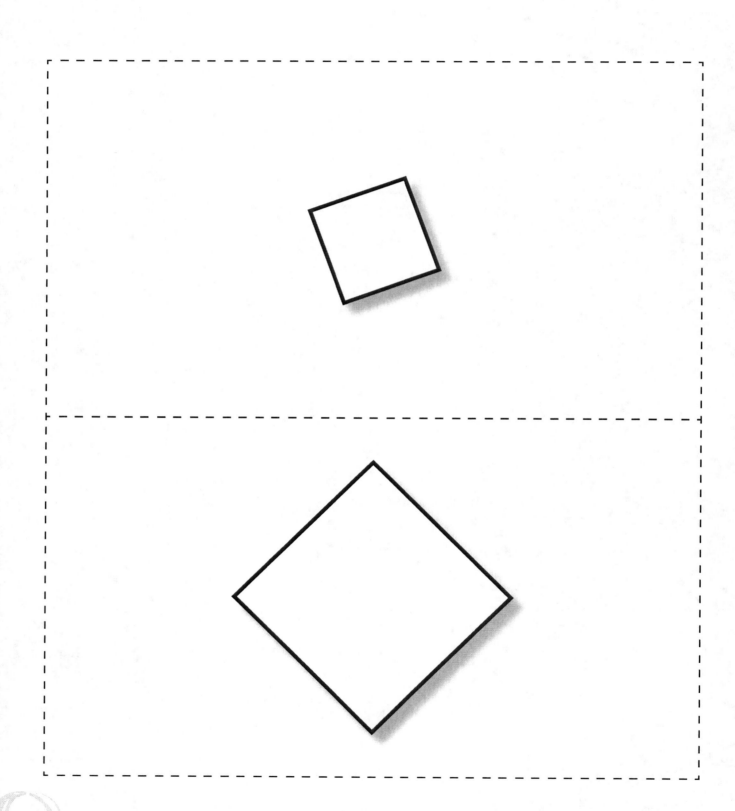

Shape Cards *(cont.)*

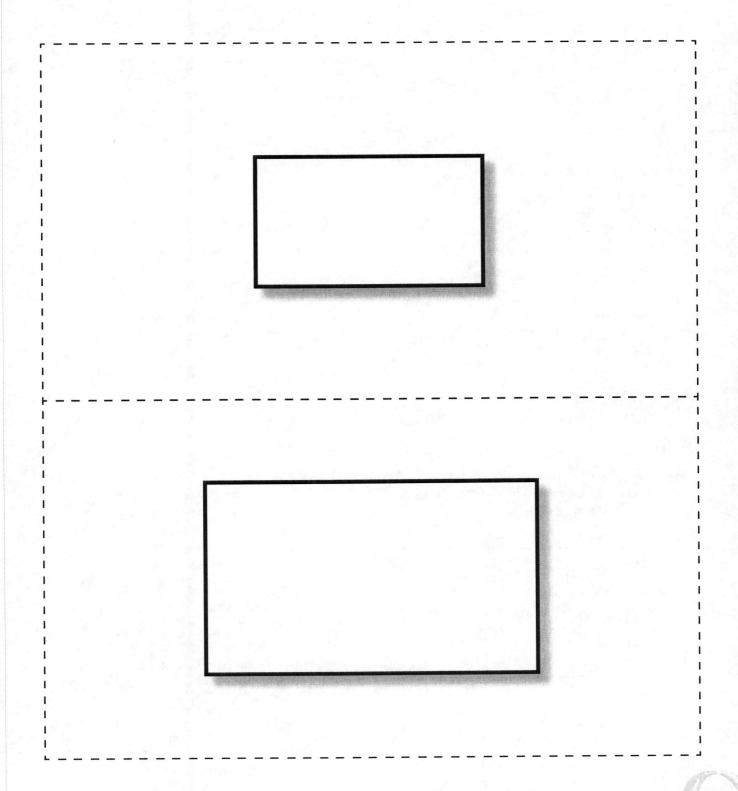

Sink or Float?

Brain-Powered Strategy	**Standard**
Sort It	Knows that different objects are made of many different types of materials and have many different observable properties

Vocabulary Words

- float
- matter
- predict
- properties
- sink

Materials

- *Matter Word Cards* (page 60)
- *Sink or Float?* (page 61)
- bucket or other large container
- real objects to observe in water
- pair of scissors
- pencil
- music

Preparation Note: Prior to the lesson, fill a bucket with water. Gather objects from around the classroom that students will use to test if they sink or float. Additionally, cut apart the *Matter Word Cards* (page 60).

Procedures

Model

1. Review with students that *matter* is what all objects are made of and that matter takes up space and has mass.

2. Explain that matter has properties that can be observed. Display the scissors and the pencil. Guide students in observing the scissors' and pencil's properties, especially the colors, shapes, and sizes. Record students' observations on the board.

3. Explain to students that they will learn about another observable property of matter.

4. Gather students around the bucket of water so they can see. Tell students that some objects sink or go to the bottom when placed in water. Place the pair of scissors in the bucket of water. Allow students to see the pair of scissors at the bottom of the bucket. Reinforce that the scissors sink in the water.

5. Tell students that some objects float when placed in water. Place the pencil in the bucket of water. Allow students to see the pencil on top of the water. Reinforce that the pencil floats in the water.

Sink or Float? *(cont.)*

Apply/Analyze

6. Distribute the *Matter Word Cards* to two students. Have one student hold the card with the word *float* on it and another student hold the card with the word *sink* on it.

7. Distribute one object to each student. Have students stand behind their chairs and name the object they were given.

8. Tell students that they will be doing a strategy called *Sort It.* (For detailed information on this strategy, see page 12.) Explain to students that they must predict if the object they have will sink or float when placed in water. Students should show their prediction by standing next to the corresponding word card.

9. Play music as students mingle around the room. Once students have sorted themselves, have them share with each other why they predicted the way they did.

10. Gather students around the bucket of water. Allow each child a turn to place his or her objects in the water and observe whether they sink or float.

11. Have students sort themselves again based on what they observed. Discuss which objects float and which sink.

Evaluate/Create

12. Distribute the *Sink or Float?* activity sheet (page 61) to students. Read the headings *Sinking* and *Floating* together as a class.

13. Ask students to draw one object that is sinking in the left glass and one object that is floating in the right. Have them share with partners why they drew the objects where they did in each glass.

14. Have each student select an object from the room. Ask them to determine if the object would most likely sink or most likely float and why. Have them share their predictions and reasoning with partners.

15. Allow students to test their predictions if possible. Students can add a picture of the object to their paper on the correct side of the paper.

Matter Word Cards

Teacher Directions: Cut apart the cards below.

sink

float

Name: _____   Date: _____

Sink or Float?

. . . .

Directions: Draw one object sinking in the glass on the left. Draw one object floating in the glass on the right. Then, explain to a partner why you drew each item in its location.

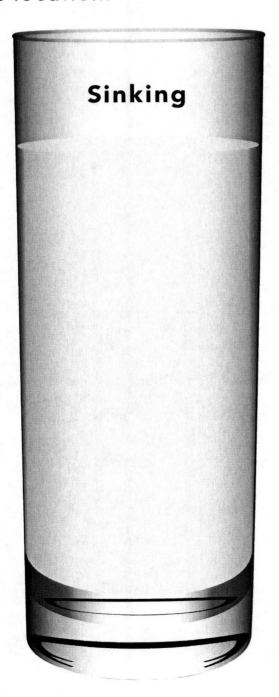

Sinking

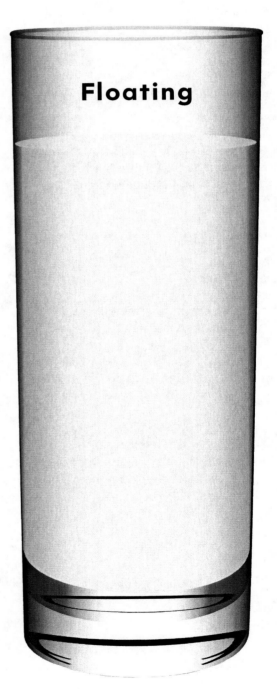

Floating

Characters: Same and Different

Brain-Powered Strategy 👥👤	Standard
It Takes Two	Describe characters, settings, and major events in a story, using key details

Vocabulary Words

- character
- comparison
- different
- same
- trait

Materials

- *Character Comparison* (page 64)
- chart paper
- story with characters that can be compared and contrasted
- sticky notes
- crayons

Preparation Note: Prior to the lesson, create a two-column chart on a sheet of chart paper. Label one of the columns *Same* and the other column *Different*.

Procedures

Model

1. Remind students that a character is a person or animal in a story.

2. Ask students to name some characters they know from books the class has read earlier in the year. Record students' responses on the board.

3. Display the cover of the selected book. Read the title and the author's name. Allow students to comment on the illustrations on the cover of the book.

4. Ask students to listen for the names of the characters and their traits as you read the story.

5. Review the characters' names at the end of the story. Discuss with students some of the traits of each character.

Characters: Same and Different (cont.)

Apply/Analyze

6. Display the previously prepared two-column chart, and distribute sticky notes to students.

7. Tell students they will be doing a strategy called *It Takes Two*. (For detailed information on this strategy, see page 13.)

8. Name two characters from the story you want students to focus on. Have students think about things that are the same and different about the characters. Have students write the word *same* or *different* at the top of the sticky note and then write or draw one trait that was either the same or different about the two characters. For example, in the story the *Three Little Pigs*, pig one and pig two are the same because they built their houses out of weak materials. If desired, write the following sentence frames on the board for students to refer to as they work:

- _____ and _____ are the same because _____.

- _____ and _____ are different because _____.

Evaluate/Create

9. Call one student at a time to place his or her sticky note on the chart in the corresponding column. Ask them to use one of the sentence frames to share orally their opinion and reasoning for their decision.

10. Distribute the *Character Comparison* activity sheet (page 64) to students.

11. Have students write a sentence stating how the characters are the same or different. Ask students to illustrate their sentences.

12. Ask students to reread the text. Have them work with partners to identify words or parts of the story that describe the characters that students wrote about. Gather students back together and discuss the words students identified.

Name: _____ Date: _____

Character Comparison

Directions: Draw and write one way the characters are alike and one way they are different.

Alike	Different

In My Opinion

Brain-Powered Strategy	Standard
It Takes Two	Write opinion pieces in which they introduce the topic or name the book they are writing about, state an opinion, supply a reason for the opinion, and provide some sense of closure

Vocabulary Words

- agree
- disagree
- opinion
- reason

Materials

- *It's a Dilemma* (page 67)
- story with a moral or dilemma (e.g., *Owen* by Kevin Henkes)
- chart paper
- two different colored markers
- sticky notes
- crayons

Preparation Note: Prior to the lesson, create a two-column chart on a sheet of chart paper. Label one of the columns *Agree* and the other column *Disagree*.

Procedures

Model

1. Write the following sentence on the board: *Two plus two equals four.*

   Write the word *fact* next to the sentence. Explain that a *fact* is something that is always true. Ask students to raise their hands if they agree with the sentence.

2. Write the following sentence on the board: *Spinach is the best food.*

   Write the word *opinion* next to the second sentence. Explain that an *opinion* is something that is true for an individual person but may or may not be true for everyone. Ask students to raise their hands if they agree with the sentence.

3. Display and discuss the cover of the storybook you will read to students. Explain that the story has a moral (or dilemma). Ask them to listen for the moral as they listen to the story and explain that the class will be discussing it together.

4. Read the book to students, stopping as needed to discuss the plot and characters. (Another option is to pause during the reading of the story after the dilemma has been introduced and complete the activity before the resolution of the book is revealed.)

In My Opinion *(cont.)*

5. Discuss the dilemma with students. Post a sheet of chart paper. In the center of the chart paper write the dilemma and draw a circle around it. Ask students to name reasons, both for and against, to agree or disagree with the dilemma. Encourage students to provide reasons from the text first. Provide the following sentence frame for students to use as they discuss their opinions: *I agree/disagree that _____ because _____.*

6. Change marker color and record reasons students may have from their own personal experiences.

Apply/Analyze

7. Display the two-column chart created prior to the lesson, and distribute sticky notes to students.

8. Tell students that they will be doing a strategy called *It Takes Two*. (For detailed information on this strategy, see page 13.)

9. Remind students about the character's dilemma in the story. Have students think about whether they agree or disagree with the dilemma. Have students write the word *agree* or *disagree* at the top of the sticky note and then write or draw one reason for their opinions. For example, in the story *Owen*, students can debate whether Owen is too old to have a blanket or not. Encourage students to use the chart the class created together for their reasons if they are stuck.

Evaluate/Create

10. Call one student at a time to place their sticky note on the chart in the corresponding column. Ask them to use one of the sentence frames to share orally their opinion and reason.

11. Distribute the *It's a Dilemma* activity sheet (page 67) to students. Have them write and draw their opinion about the dilemma from the story. Remind students they may change their opinion or reason based on what other students shared when putting their sticky notes on the chart.

12. Have students with the same opinions form groups. Ask each group to discuss the reasons each student used to support his or her idea. Have the group decide which reason provides the most support for the opinion and why. Allow each group to share its opinion and their strongest reason.

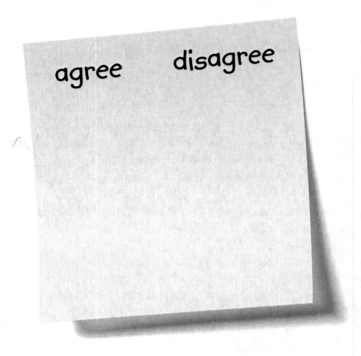

Name: _____   Date: _____

It's a Dilemma

. . . .

Directions: Draw and write about the dilemma in the book you read. Do you agree or disagree?

_____

- -

_____

- -

_____

- -

_____

- -

_____

Is Bigger Better?

Brain-Powered Strategy	**Standard**
It Takes Two	Order three objects by length; compare the lengths of two objects indirectly by using a third object

Vocabulary Words	**Materials**
• compare • larger • size • smaller	• chart paper • playground ball • objects from around the room for size comparison • sticky notes

Preparation Note: Prior to the lesson, create a two-column chart on a sheet of chart paper. Label one of the columns *Larger Than* and the other column *Smaller Than*.

Procedures

Model

1. Call one student to the front of the room. Ask students to describe the student's height. Accept all reasonable answers.

2. Stand next to the student and ask students to describe the student's height again compared to your height. Guide students to understand that two objects help provide a comparison point and make it easier to accurately describe the size of both objects.

3. Hold up a playground ball or other object. Tell students that the ball could be described as large or small. Remind students of the activity in Steps 1–2 and that the size of the ball can more accurately be described by comparing it to other objects.

4. Look around the classroom for an object that is smaller than the playground ball. Hold one object in each hand. Show students the smaller object and tell them the object is smaller than the ball.

5. Write the following sentence frame on the board, and use it to compare the two objects: *The (ball) is smaller than the _____.* Find several other objects from around the room that are smaller than the ball, if needed.

6. Look around the classroom for an object that is larger than the playground ball and repeat Steps 4–5 with the larger object and the following sentence frame: *The _____ is larger than the (ball).*

Is Bigger Better? *(cont.)*

Apply/Analyze

7. Display the previously prepared two-column chart, and distribute sticky notes to students.

8. Tell students that they will be doing a strategy called *It Takes Two*. (For detailed information on this strategy, see page 13.)

9. Have students find an object in the room, and draw a picture of it on the sticky note. Then, display an object for students to use as a size comparison. Students must determine if the object they drew is larger than or smaller than the object you displayed.

Evaluate/Create

10. Call one student at a time to place his or her sticky note on the chart in the correct column. Ask them to use one of the sentence frames to share orally their size comparison. You may want students to actually bring the object to the front of the room as they are sharing so there is a physical comparison.

11. Repeat the activity as needed, displaying different objects for comparison each time.

12. Have students retrieve their sticky notes, or if possible, hold the real object. Arrange students into groups of three to five. Ask the groups to work together to arrange their objects in order from largest to smallest. Allow several groups to share their sequencing and how they determined where each person would stand.

Nouns and Verbs

Brain-Powered Strategy	Standard
ABC Professors	Use singular and plural nouns with matching verbs in basic sentences

Vocabulary Words	Materials
• noun • plural • singular • verb	• *ABC Professor Notes* (page 72) • poster boards or chart paper • writing paper

Preparation Note: Prior to the lesson, create two poster-size versions of the *ABC Professor Notes* activity sheet (page 72). This can be done on a piece of poster board or a large sheet of chart paper.

Procedures

Model

1. Choose one student to come to the front of the room. Ask the other students to name the chosen student. Remind students that a boy or girl is a person, which can also be called a *noun*. Also, remind students that places and things are called *nouns*.

2. Whisper an action in the student's ear, such as swim. Have the student pantomime swimming. Have the rest of the class guess what the action is. Remind students that *verbs* are action words.

3. Review with students the difference between singular nouns and plural nouns and the corresponding verb tense.

4. Tell students that they will be doing a strategy called *ABC Professors*. (For detailed information on this strategy, see page 14.)

5. Display the poster-size version of the *ABC Professor Notes* activity sheet. Write the word *nouns* at the top of this poster. Begin with the letter *A* and model naming several nouns beginning with the letter *A*, for example: *apple*, *ant*, *astronaut*, and *arrow*. Model several more boxes for students, as needed.

6. Display the second poster-sized version of the *ABC Professor Notes* activity sheet. Write the word *verbs* at the top of the poster. Choose another letter to begin with, such as *S*, and model naming several verbs that begin with the letter *S*, for example: *swim*, *slide*, and *swallow*. Model several more boxes for students, as needed.

Nouns and Verbs *(cont.)*

7. Model how to create sentences using a noun from the noun chart and a verb from the verb chart. The sentences can be silly or serious. Discuss with students the difference between singular and plural nouns and how that affects the verb. For example: *The astronaut swims* and *Six astronauts swim.*

Apply/Analyze

8. Divide students into two groups. Assign one group the nouns, and assign the other group the verbs. Distribute the *ABC Professor Notes* activity sheet (page 72) to each student. An enlarged version of this chart can be found on the Digital Resource CD (filename: abcprofessornotes.pdf).

9. Ask the groups to work together to complete the chart with their assigned words. Students can write more than one word in each box.

10. Gather students back together and have groups share their words aloud.

Evaluate/Create

11. Distribute writing paper to students.

12. Ask students to choose one word from the noun poster and one word from the verb poster.

13. Have students write a sentence using the noun in singular form and the matching verb.

14. Have students write a second sentence using the same noun and verb, but this time, the noun should be in plural form with the matching verb.

15. Provide students with three sentences, and have them discuss with a partner why the noun and verb match or do not match. Be sure they justify their answers. If they disagree, have them put a star by the sentence. Discuss each as a class sharing their reasoning.

Aa

Name: _____ Date: _____

ABC Professor Notes

Directions: Think of a noun or a verb. What letter does that word start with? Find that box and write the word or draw a picture of it in the box.

A	B	C	D	E
F	G	H	I	J
K	L	M	N	O
P	Q	R	S	T
U	V	W	X	Y
Z				

 #51178—*Brain-Powered Lessons to Engage All Learners*

Wonderful Weather

Brain-Powered Strategy	**Standard**
ABC Professors	Knows that short-term weather conditions can change daily and weather patterns change over the seasons

Vocabulary Words	**Materials**
• weather	• *ABC Professor Notes* (page 75)
	• *Relating Weather* (page 76)
	• crayons

Preparation Note: Prior to the lesson, create a poster-size version of the *ABC Professor Notes* activity sheet (page 75).

Procedures

Model

1. Sing the song "The Itsy Bitsy Spider" with students.

2. Ask students to identify the two types of weather mentioned in the song—rainy and sunny. Explain to students that the class will study a science unit on weather.

3. Tell students that they will be doing a strategy called *ABC Professors*. (For detailed information on this strategy, see page 14.)

4. Display the poster-size version of the *ABC Professor Notes* activity sheet. Tell students that they will be practicing using the activity sheet on a topic they know a lot about and that is not related to the lesson.

5. Model for students how to think of a food item, such as an *apple*. Sound out the word *apple* and identify that since it starts with the letter *a*, it will go in the box with the letter *A*. Model either drawing a picture of an apple or writing the word *apple* in the box with the letter *A*.

6. Ask for several students to volunteer food items to place in different boxes on the poster.

Wonderful Weather (cont.)

Apply/Analyze

7. Distribute the *ABC Professor Notes* activity sheet to students. An enlarged version of this chart can be found on the Digital Resource CD (filename: abcprofessornotes. pdf).

8. Ask students to complete as many of the boxes as they can with words that tell about the weather. Students may draw pictures or write words. They may also write more than one word in each box.

9. Save students' activity sheets until you have completed the unit of study.

Evaluate/Create

10. Distribute either the same *ABC Professor Notes* activity sheet students had previously filled out at the beginning of the unit of study, or provide them with a blank version.

11. Have students complete as many of the boxes as they can with words that tell about the weather. Use the activity sheet as an evaluation of what students learned during the weather unit.

12. Distribute the *Relating Weather* activity sheet (page 76) to students. Ask students to choose three related words from the *ABC Professor Notes* activity sheet and write about how these words relate to each other.

Name: _____   Date: _____

ABC Professor Notes

Directions: Think of a word that relates to weather. What letter does that word start with? Find that box and write the word or draw a picture of it in the box.

A	B	C	D	E
F	G	H	I	J
K	L	M	N	O
P	Q	R	S	T
U	V	W	X	Y
Z				

Name: _____   Date: _____

Relating Weather

Directions: Choose three related words from the *ABC Professor Notes* activity sheet. Write about how those words relate to one another. Then, draw a picture.

Life Long Ago

Brain-Powered Strategy	**Standard**
ABC Professors	Understands changes in community over time

Vocabulary Words

- change
- community
- long ago

Materials

- *ABC Professor Notes* (page 79)
- *Long Ago and Now* (page 80)
- poster board or chart paper
- photos depicting change in a community over time (*optional*)
- crayons

Preparation Note: Prior to the lesson, create a poster-size version of the *ABC Professor Notes* activity sheet (page 79). You may wish to complete this activity throughout the course of a unit of study on life long ago. Allow students to keep their own copies of the *ABC Professor Notes* activity sheet at their desks if they are capable of updating it, or consider keeping a class version on a large poster board or sheet of chart paper.

Procedures

Model

1. Tell students that they will be doing a strategy called *ABC Professors*. (For detailed information on this strategy, see page 14.)

2. Distribute the *ABC Professor Notes* activity sheet to students. Tell students that they will use the activity sheet to better understand some changes that have occurred in the community over time.

3. Model for students how change has occurred within a community. For example, methods of transportation have changed over the years. Write the word *transportation* in the appropriate box of the *ABC Professor Notes* activity sheet. If desired, show photos depicting the changes that have occurred over the years.

4. Ask several students to share additional ideas, and record their answers in the appropriate boxes.

5. Have students work individually, in partners, or in small groups to think of a word or phrase for each letter of the alphabet.

Life Long Ago *(cont.)*

Apply/Analyze

6. Display the poster version of the *ABC Professor Notes* activity sheet.

7. Tell students that throughout the class's unit of study on life long ago, they will help to choose a word or phrase for each letter of the alphabet.

8. Assist students in adding to the chart throughout your unit of study on life long ago.

Evaluate/Create

9. Distribute the *Long Ago and Now* activity sheet (page 80) to students.

10. Have students choose one word from the *ABC Professor Notes* poster. Ask students to draw or write about their understanding of the word or phrase as it relates to long ago on the top. Have students draw or write about the word or phrase as it relates to how it has changed over time on the bottom. Ask students to determine why the change has been made in the community. For example, students may draw a dirt road at the top of the page and a paved road at the bottom of the page and determine that cars are able to travel easier on paved roads.

11. Allow students to share their writing, illustrations, and reasoning with partners or choose a few students to share with the whole class.

There Is Support

Brain-Powered Strategy	**Standard**
Kinesthetic Word Webs	Identify the main topic and retell key details of a text

Vocabulary Words	**Materials**
• details	• *Topic and Detail Cards* (pages 83–88)
• main topic	• index cards
• retell	• chart paper
• support	• tape
• topic	• sheet of paper or sentence strip
	• writing paper

Preparation Note: Prior to the lesson, think of several sentences about yourself that your students will recognize about you as a teacher and several about yourself that are not related to teaching. Write each sentence on a separate index card. Additionally, cut apart the *Topic and Detail Cards* (pages 83–88).

Procedures

Model

1. Write the following sentence on a sheet of chart paper: _____ *is a teacher.* Ask students to think about you as a teacher.

2. Tell students that you will read some sentences to them. If they think a sentence tells about you as a teacher, they should show a thumbs-up. If they do not think the sentence tells about you as a teacher, they should show a thumbs-down. Read the index cards with sentences about you.

3. Refer back to the sentence you wrote on the chart paper. Tell students that this sentence is called the *topic*. It tells about what the rest of the sentences will be about.

4. Tape the index cards with sentences that tell about you as a teacher under the sentence you wrote on the chart paper. Explain that the sentences that come after the topic sentence are *details* and they support or tell more about the topic sentence.

5. Cover up the topic sentence on the chart paper with a sheet of paper or a sentence strip, and write the following topic sentence in its place: *Ice cream is my favorite food.* Explain that the topic sentence tells about ice cream, but all the sentences that follow tell about you as a teacher.

There Is Support (cont.)

6. Uncover the original topic sentence and emphasize that the topic and details once again match. The topic sentence is about you as a teacher and all the sentences that follow tell about you as a teacher.

Apply/Analyze

7. Tell students that they will be doing a strategy called *Kinesthetic Word Webs*. (For detailed information on this strategy, see page 15.)

8. Distribute the *Topic and Detail Cards* to students. You may wish to use enlarged versions of these cards that are found on the Digital Resource CD (filename: topicdetailcards.pdf).

9. Instruct students to walk around the room looking for topic and detail sentences that belong together.

10. Once a group of students believes they have found the topic and all of the details in the web, instruct them to form an outer circle and have the student holding the topic sentence card stand in the middle. The outer circle of students should place one hand on the shoulder of the student with the topic sentence card, creating a *Kinesthetic Word Web*.

11. Debrief with students by discussing questions such as the ones listed below. Then, have each group read aloud their topic sentence followed by the details.

- How did you know where you belong?

- What is the main topic of your group?

- What are some supporting details?

Evaluate/Create

12. Distribute writing paper to students, and write the following topic sentence on the board: *My favorite food is _____.* Have students copy the topic sentence on their papers including filling in the blank with the names of their favorite foods.

13. Provide time for students to write two detail sentences. The sentences should support the topic sentence.

14. Have students form pairs. Ask one student to read his or her topic sentence and the two supporting detail sentences. Have the partner decide which detail sentence they think fits best with the topic sentence, and explain why. Have partners switch roles.

Topic and Detail Cards

Teacher Directions: Cut apart the cards below.

There are many fun things to do at recess.

Going down the slide is fun.

Jump ropes are out for kids to jump.

Balls can be used to play handball.

Topic and Detail Cards *(cont.)*

The stem holds up the leaves.

Leaves make food for plants.

Plants have many parts.

Roots bring water into plants.

Topic and Detail Cards *(cont.)*

My cousin is a great friend to me.

She always shares with me.

We love to play board games together.

We like to tell each other secrets.

Topic and Detail Cards *(cont.)*

Summer is the best season of all.

Swimming is a fun activity.

There is no school.

We eat lots of popsicles.

Topic and Detail Cards (cont.)

My weekend was fun.

I got to stay up late Friday night.

I went to my friend's house on Saturday.

My family went to the movies on Sunday.

Topic and Detail Cards *(cont.)*

A square
has special
features.

It has four
sides.

Each side
is equal
in length.

It has four
corners.

Elaborate with Details

Brain-Powered Strategy	Standard
Kinesthetic Word Webs	With guidance and support from adults, focus on a topic, respond to questions and suggestions from peers, and add details to strengthen writing as needed

Vocabulary Words	Materials
• details • topic	• *Sentence Cards* (pages 91–93) • *Five W Cards* (pages 94–96) • writing paper • teacher-selected text for students to analyze

Preparation Note: Prior to the lesson, cut apart the *Sentence Cards* (pages 91–93) and the *Five W Cards* (pages 94–96).

Procedures

Model

1. Ask students to give two people a high five. Tell students that hand gestures will help them with their writing today.

2. Draw a picture of the outline of a hand on the board. Write the following words next to the fingers, one word per finger: *who, what, where, why,* and *when.*

3. Have students practice wiggling each finger as they name the five words.

4. Write the following sentence on the board: *The woman wore a dress.* Read the sentence to students and explain that the sentence does not tell much information.

5. Refer back to the outline of the hand with the five question words. Explain that those words will help add detail or tell more about the sentence to make it more interesting.

6. Model adding more detail to the existing sentence that answers each of the questions. For example: *The old woman wore a fancy dress to the wedding of her granddaughter last night.* If desired, answer only one or two of the questions in the original sentence and add additional sentences. For example: *The old woman wore a fancy dress. Her granddaughter got married last night. The woman shopped for months to find just the right dress to wear.*

Elaborate with Details *(cont.)*

Apply/Analyze

7. Tell students that they will be doing a strategy called *Kinesthetic Word Webs.* (For detailed information on this strategy, see page 15.)

8. Provide students with the *Sentence Cards* and the *Five W Cards.* You may wish to use enlarged versions of these cards that are found on the Digital Resource CD (filenames: sentencecards.pdf and fivewcards.pdf).Be sure to have each of the five question cards for each sentence.

9. Instruct students to walk around the room and form groups that include one sentence card and each of the five question cards.

10. Once a group of students has a sentence and five question cards, instruct them to form an outer circle, and have the student holding the sentence card stand in the middle. The outer circle of students should each place one hand on the shoulder of the student with the topic sentence card, creating a *Kinesthetic Word Web.*

11. Have students work together to provide details to the sentence by expanding the sentence or adding sentences to answer each of the question cards. Distribute the writing paper to students, and have them record their sentences on their paper.

12. Gather the class back together and have each group read aloud their sentence.

13. Debrief with students by discussing questions, such as the following:

- How did answering the questions add details to the original sentence?

- Which question words were easy/hard to answer and include in the original sentence?

14. Provide students with a teacher-selected text, and assign a sentence or a paragraph to read. Have students identify which of the five *W*s are represented in the text and which ones are not.

15. Discuss with students what they would add to the text to answer the missing question or questions.

Evaluate/Create

16. Write each of the sentences from the *Sentence Cards* on the board.

17. Have students choose a sentence and write it at the top of their writing paper. Students should then work to write a more detailed sentence(s) that answers some of the five questions.

18. Choose a student to share his or her sentence with the whole class. Write it on the board if needed. Have the other students in the class determine the answers to as many of the questions as were answered in the student's sentence.

19. Work together as a class to determine which of the five *W* questions could be removed from the sentence without changing the meaning of the sentence.

Sentence Cards

Teacher Directions: Cut apart the cards below.

The dog ran.	**We went to the movies.**
He drove his car.	**She had fun.**

Sentence Cards *(cont.)*

Mom cooked dinner.

Dad played ball.

Sam read a book.

Nancy is her friend.

Sentence Cards *(cont.)*

The phone rang.

They came.

The robot walks.

He rides.

Five *W* Cards

Teacher Directions: Cut apart the cards below.

who

who

what

what

Five *W* Cards (cont.)

where

where

why

why

Five *W* Cards <small>*(cont.)*</small>

when

when

Number Representations

Brain-Powered Strategy	Standard
Kinesthetic Word Webs	Apply properties of operations as strategies to add

Vocabulary Words	Materials
• addition • number model • representation	• *Number Representation Cards* (pages 99–104) • *Number Representation Web* (page 105) • index cards • chart paper

Preparation Note: Prior to the lesson, cut apart the *Number Representation Cards* (pages 99–104).

Procedures

Model

1. Distribute index cards to students. Ask them to draw one object of their choosing on the index card.

2. Collect the index cards, and display them for the class. Discuss with students how they were all able to show the number one, but they may have chosen a different way or different object to do so.

3. Write the number 11 in the center of a sheet of chart paper. Draw a circle around it.

4. Tell students that there are many ways to show the number 11. Create a web around the center circle by sharing with students the following ways to show 11:

   • Eleven tally marks

   • The word *eleven*

   • Eleven stars

   • One ten frame and one single unit

   • 10 + 1

5. Circle each way to make 11 as you add it to the chart paper. Draw a line back to the center circle to show the relationship.

6. Encourage students to suggest additional ways to show 11.

Apply/Analyze

7. Tell students that they will be doing a strategy called *Kinesthetic Word Webs*. (For detailed information on this strategy, see page 15.)

8. Provide students with the *Number Representation Cards*. You may wish to use enlarged versions of these cards that are found on the Digital Resource CD (filename: numbercards.pdf).

9. Instruct students to walk around the room looking for number representations related to the one on their cards.

Number Representations (cont.)

10. Once a group of students believes they have found all of the numbers in the web, instruct them to form an outer circle and have the student holding the numeral card stand in the middle. The outer circle of students should each place one hand on the shoulder of the student with the numeral card, creating a *Kinesthetic Word Web*.

11. Debrief with students by discussing questions, such as the following:

- How did you know where you belong?

- Are there other ways to represent the number?

Evaluate/Create

12. Distribute the *Number Representation Web* activity sheet (page 105) to students. Assign students numbers, or have students choose their own numbers to write in the middle of the web.

13. Have students write at least four different representations of the number on the web.

14. Group students into pairs. Ask students to compare their two numbers to determine which number is more and which number is less. Have students select one of the representations they made and be ready to explain how they arrived at their decision.

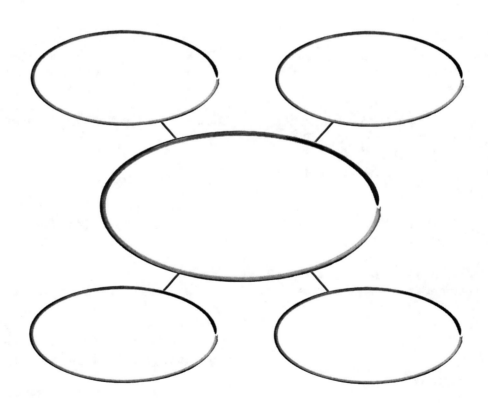

Number Representation Cards

Teacher Directions: Cut apart the cards below.

8

eight

6 + 2

Number Representation Cards (cont.)

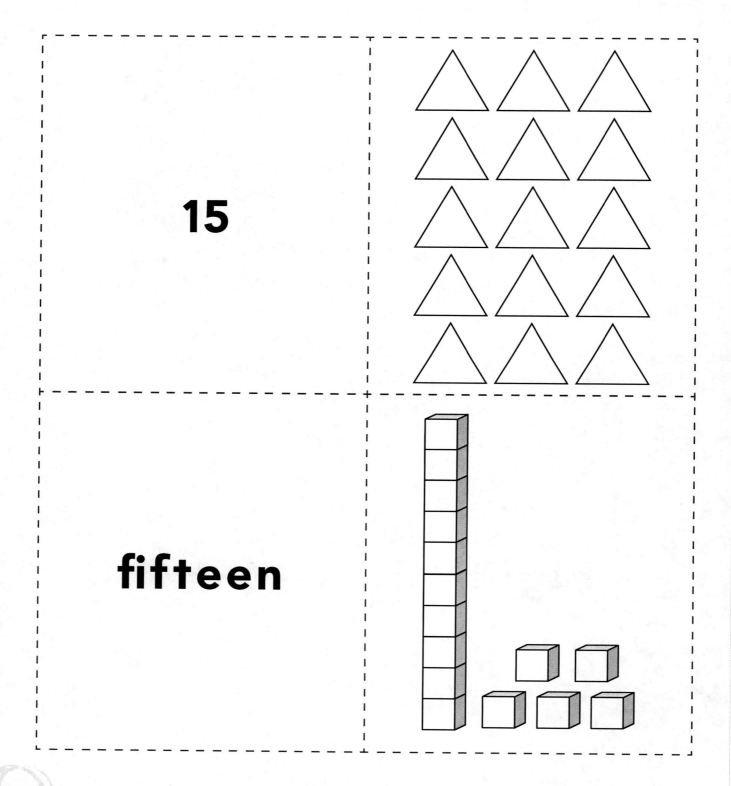

15

fifteen

Number Representation Cards *(cont.)*

20

twenty

Number Representation Cards (cont.)

25

20 + 5

twenty-five

Number Representation Cards *(cont.)*

28

20 + 8

twenty-eight

Number Representation Cards (cont.)

31

30 + 1

thirty-one

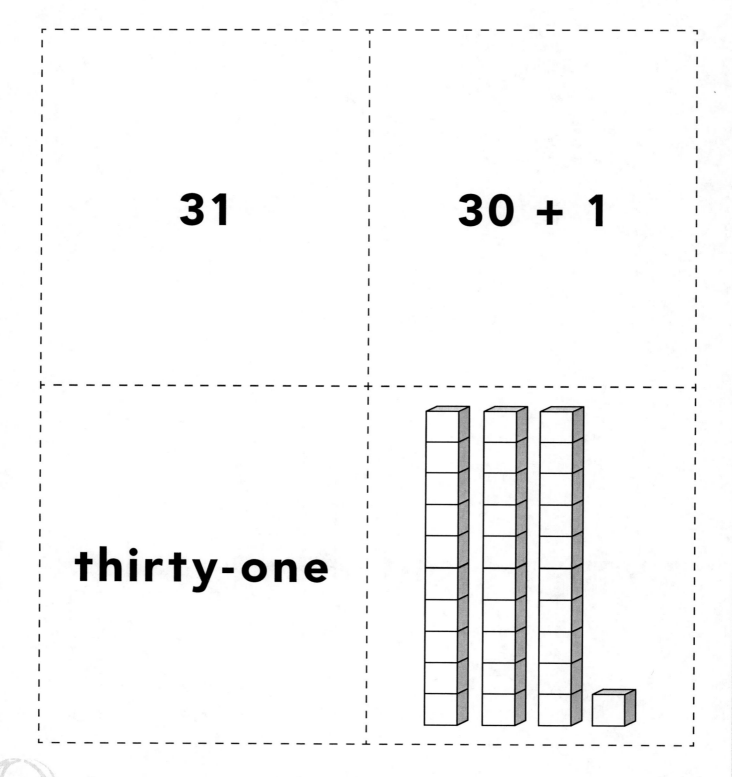

Name: _____ Date: _____

Number Representation Web

Directions: Write your chosen number or the number assigned to you in the center oval. In the outside ovals, draw or write different representations of that number.

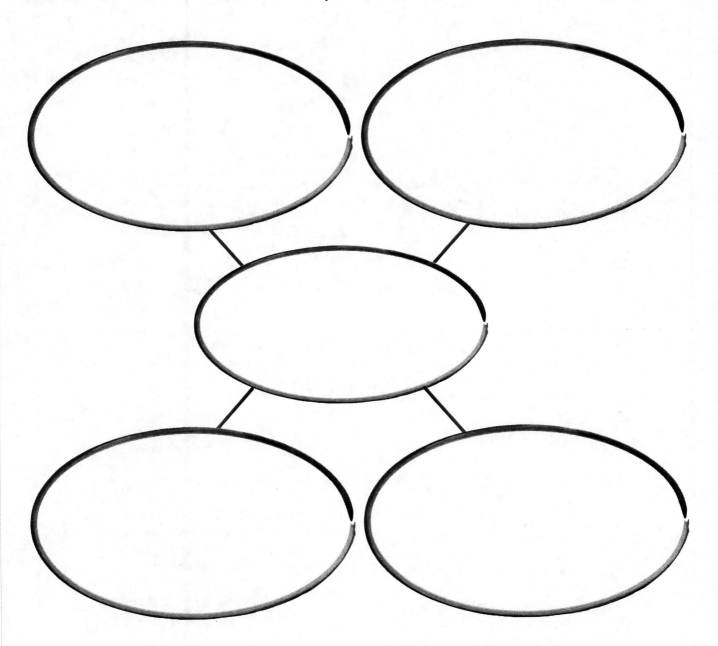

Goods and Services

Brain-Powered Strategy	**Standard**
Kinesthetic Word Webs	Knows that goods are objects that can satisfy people's wants, and services are activities that can satisfy people's wants

Vocabulary Words

- good
- need
- service
- want

Materials

- *Goods and Services Cards* (pages 108–113)
- chart paper
- crayons
- scissors

Preparation Note: Prior to the lesson, create a two-column chart on a sheet of chart paper. Write the word *Goods* on one side and *Services* on the other side. Additionally, cut apart the *Goods and Services Cards* (pages 108–113).

Procedures

Model

1. Name the items listed below. Ask students to name where they would go in the community to get each item. Students may provide several store names for each item.

   - lettuce
   - a haircut
   - a shirt
   - fix a broken car

2. Display the previously prepared two-column chart. Explain to students that *goods* are things that people grow or make. Hold up the box of crayons and tell students that the crayons are a good. A factory made the crayons, and you went to a store to buy them. Write the word *crayons* in the goods column. Provide several other examples, as needed.

3. Have students name other goods that are grown or made by people. Add those items to the list.

4. Explain to students that *services* are jobs people do to help others. Hold up the pair of scissors. Explain to students that when you go to the salon to get your hair cut, you are getting a service. The hairstylist's job is to cut your hair. Emphasize that services are activities that people do, not usually physical objects. Write the word *haircut* in the services column. Provide several other examples, as needed.

5. Have students name other services. Add those items to the list.

Goods and Services *(cont.)*

Apply/Analyze

6. Tell students that they will be doing a strategy called *Kinesthetic Word Webs*. (For detailed information on this strategy, see page 15.)

7. Distribute the *Goods and Services Cards*, one to each student. You may wish to use enlarged versions of these cards that are found on the Digital Resource CD (filename: goodsservicescards.pdf).

8. Instruct students to walk around the room looking to match pictures of goods with the word card that says *goods* and the pictures of services with the word card that says *services*.

9. Once a group of students believes it has found all of the goods and services, instruct them to form an outer circle and have the student holding the word cards stand in the middle. The outer circle of students should each place one hand on the shoulder of the student with the word cards, creating a *Kinesthetic Word Web*.

10. Debrief with students by discussing questions, such as the following:

- How did you know where you belong?

- What are some goods and services that are a part of your group?

Have the student web with the goods say aloud each of the goods in their group. Repeat with the services group.

11. Have students determine if the card they are holding is a want or a need and why. Allow each student to share his or her good or service and rationale for whether it is a want or a need.

Evaluate/Create

12. Divide students into pairs or triads. Have the groups determine a service that someone can provide and a good that would be needed to provide that service. For example, a barber provides the service of cutting hair but needs shampoo in order to provide his service.

13. Ask the groups to determine if the services and goods are wants or needs and why.

14. Have each group share aloud for the whole class to hear its services and goods pairing and whether it is a want or need.

Goods and Services Cards

Teacher Directions: Cut apart the cards below.

Goods

Goods and Services Cards *(cont.)*

Goods and Services Cards (cont.)

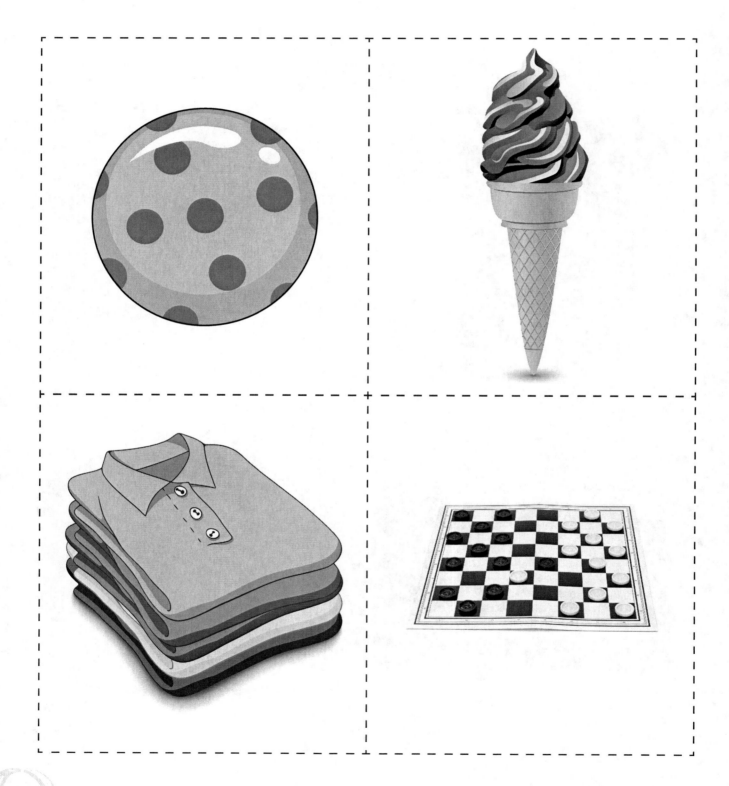

Goods and Services Cards *(cont.)*

Services

Goods and Services Cards (cont.)

Goods and Services Cards (cont.)

What Does It Mean?

Brain-Powered Strategy	Standard
Matchmaker	With guidance and support from adults, demonstrate understanding of word relationships and nuances in word meanings

Vocabulary Words	Materials
• definition • meaning • vocabulary	• *It's My Word* (page 116) • book with rich vocabulary • index cards • pocket chart (*optional*) • crayon • tape

Procedures

Model

1. Explain to students that you will read a story to them that has some vocabulary in it they may not know.

2. Teach them the following sign to show you that they do not know a word. Have students bend their elbows and put their palms up. Once in this position, students can shrug their shoulders to indicate "I don't know." Practice several times.

3. Introduce the book to students by displaying and discussing the cover with them. Read the title and author's name, and have students make predictions about what the story will be about.

4. Remind students of the sign for not knowing a word. Explain to them that they should show that sign if there is a word they do not know, and you will stop to explain its definition.

5. Read the story to students, pausing each time they show you the sign for an unknown word. Write each unknown word on an index card. As you explain the definition of the word, write the definition on another index card.

6. Display the vocabulary word and the matching definition in a pocket chart or on the board. Discuss possible word relationships and nuances between the words with students.

7. Develop students' understanding of the words by asking questions about the words. Vary the questions according to the vocabulary words. For example:

   • Which word would you use to describe a person?

   • Which word tells how someone feels?

What Does It Mean? *(cont.)*

Apply/Analyze

8. Tell students that they will be doing a strategy in which they make a model called a *Matchmaker*. (For detailed information on this strategy, see page 16.)

9. Distribute the vocabulary index cards to students. **Note:** Not every student may receive an index card. Have students who receive a card attach it to their shirts using tape.

10. Have students stand in a circle. Place the index cards with the definitions on them on the floor randomly in the center of the circle.

11. Ask students to pick up the cards from the center of the circle but not the card that matches their vocabulary word.

12. Have students hold hands around the circle as they also hold the card they picked up. Students must get the definition card to the person wearing the matching vocabulary card without letting go of their hands.

13. Allow students to not hold hands if needed. However, the energy level and engagement level increases with the challenge of holding hands and moving the cards around the circle.

14. Have each student read the vocabulary words and the matching definitions aloud once as he or she has matched all the cards. The rest of the group can agree or disagree and, if needed, move the cards to the correct person.

Evaluate/Create

15. Distribute the *It's My Word* activity sheet (page 116) to students.

16. Have each student write a word at the top of the activity sheet. Ask students to illustrate a picture that helps show the definition. Then, have them write sentences using the selected words.

17. Pair students together randomly. Ask pairs of students to discuss their two vocabulary words and determine if the words are related in any way or not. Have students be prepared to share their words and reasoning with the whole group.

Name: _____   Date: _____

It's My Word

Directions: Write your vocabulary word. Draw a picture to show the meaning of your word. Then, write a sentence using your word.

Word — — — — — — — — — — — — — — — — —

It Represents the U.S.

Brain-Powered Strategy

Matchmaker

Standards

Knows the history of American symbols

Knows why important buildings, statues, and monuments are associated with state and national history

Vocabulary Words

- liberty
- memorial
- monument
- symbol

Materials

- *Symbols Picture Cards* (pages 119–121)
- *Symbols Definition Cards* (pages 122–124)
- book about national symbols and monuments (e.g., *O, Say Can You See? America's Symbols, Landmarks, and Important Words* by Sheila Keenan)
- tape
- grade-level informational text on an American symbol or a landmark

Preparation Note: Prior to the lesson, cut apart the *Symbols Picture Cards* (pages 119–121). Make enough copies for each student to receive one. Additionally, cut apart the *Symbols Definition Cards* (pages 122–124), and make enough corresponding definitions to the *Symbols Picture Cards.*

Procedures

Model

1. Review the symbols and monuments of the United States by reading a book on the topic.

2. Discuss with students symbols and monuments they are most familiar and least familiar with. Review symbols that students are unfamiliar with.

3. Draw a dollar sign on the board. Tell students that the dollar sign is a symbol for money. When we see the dollar sign, we know that it stands for money.

4. Explain that the United States has many symbols that stand for things important to the United States.

It Represents the U.S. *(cont.)*

5. Tell students that our country also has buildings and monuments that remind us of important events and people in history. When we see them, we are reminded of the freedom we have as a country.

Apply/Analyze

6. Tell students that they will be doing an activity in which they make a model called a *Matchmaker*. (For detailed information on this strategy, see page 16.)

7. Distribute the *Symbols Picture Cards* to students. You may wish to use enlarged versions of these cards and the *Symbols Definitions Cards* found on the Digital Resource CD (filename: symbolcards.pdf and definitioncards.pdf). Have each student attach the card to his or her shirt using tape.

8. Have students stand in a circle. Place the *Symbols Definitions Cards* on the floor randomly in the center of the circle.

9. Ask students to pick up the cards from the center of the circle, but not their own card.

10. Have students hold hands around the circle as they also hold the card they picked up. Students must get the definition card to the person wearing the matching picture card without letting go of their hands.

11. Allow students to not hold hands if needed. However, the energy level and engagement level increases with the challenge of holding hands and moving the cards around the circle.

12. Have students read the definitions and matching picture cards aloud once they have matched all the cards. The rest of the group can agree or disagree and, if needed, move the cards to the correct person.

Evaluate/Create

13. Provide students with informational text about an American symbol. Read the text together as a class.

14. Have students work with partners to identify words that identify why the American symbol stands for freedom. Gather the class together and discuss the words students identified.

Symbols Picture Cards

Teacher Directions: Cut apart the cards below.

American Flag

Mount Rushmore

Liberty Bell

Capitol

Symbols Picture Cards *(cont.)*

Bald Eagle

Lincoln Memorial

George Washington

Statue of Liberty

Symbols Picture Cards *(cont.)*

Star-Spangled Banner

Ellis Island

World War II Memorial

The White House

Symbols Definition Cards

Teacher Directions: Cut apart the cards below.

This symbol has 50 stars and 13 stripes. Its colors are red, white, and blue.

This monument of the faces of four presidents is carved into the side of a mountain.

This bell is located in Philadelphia and is a symbol of freedom.

This building is where Congress meets.

Symbols Definition Cards *(cont.)*

This national bird symbolizes strength, freedom, and courage.

This statue honors the 16th president, Abraham Lincoln.

This first president is also known as the "Father of our Country."

This statue is located in New York Harbor and is a symbol of freedom.

Symbols Definition Cards *(cont.)*

People stand to show respect when they hear this national song being played.

This is an island families had to stop at when entering the United States from other countries.

This memorial reminds us of the men and women who fought in World War II.

This is the house where the president and his family live.

Character Connections

Brain-Powered Strategy	**Standard**
Just Say It	Compare and contrast the adventures and experiences of characters in stories

Vocabulary Words

- character
- compare
- contrast

Materials

- *Character Compare and Contrast* (page 127)
- two different types of balls (e.g., soccer ball, basketball)
- chart paper
- two stories with characters that have adventures or experiences that can be compared and contrasted
- crayons

Procedures

Model

1. Display the two balls, and have students name them. Ask students to tell how the balls are the same. Record student responses on the sheet of chart paper.

2. Ask students to tell how the two balls are different. Record student responses.

3. Explain to students that when they tell how things are the same, they are *comparing* the two items. Review the comparing responses on the sheet of chart paper.

4. Explain to students that when they tell how things are different, they are *contrasting* the two items. Review the contrasting responses on the sheet of chart paper.

5. Display the cover of the first book you will read to students. Read the title and author of the book. Name the character you want students to pay close attention to in the story.

6. Ensure students understand the adventures or experiences the character has after you are done reading the book. Students can simply retell the story to partners, or a more elaborate lesson can be done by mapping the sequence of events using a graphic organizer prior to the *Apply/Analyze* section of this lesson.

7. Repeat Steps 5–6 with the second book.

Character Connections *(cont.)*

Apply/Analyze

8. Tell students that they will be doing an activity called *Just Say It*. (For detailed information on this strategy, see page 17.)

9. Group students into pairs. Have the two students face each other and identify one as Partner *A* and the other as Partner *B*.

10. Tell students that you want them to compare the two characters by telling things that are the same about them. Have Partner *A* share his or her ideas with Partner *B*. Partner *B* should only listen during this time.

11. Provide Partner *B* 30 seconds to respond to what Partner *A* shared. Encourage students to either add new information or help provide more detail to the comments Partner *A* shared. Partner *A* should listen attentively.

12. Have partners switch roles and allow Partner *B* to contrast the two characters for 30 seconds before allowing Partner *A* to respond.

Evaluate/Create

13. Distribute the *Character Compare and Contrast* activity sheet (page 127) to students. Have students write and draw one adventure or experience the characters had that was the same and one adventure or experience that was different.

14. Have students share their writing with their partners.

15. Ask partners to discuss if they have had any of the same adventures or experiences that the characters they compared and contrasted had. Allow several students to share experiences that were the same.

Name: _____   Date: _____

Character Compare and Contrast

Directions: Write the names of the two characters from the two stories. Draw one way they are alike. Draw one way they are different.

Character 1 _____

Character 2 _____

Compare

Contrast

Expanding Details

Brain-Powered Strategy	**Standard**
Just Say It	Write informative/explanatory texts in which they name a topic, supply some facts about the topic, and provide some sense of closure

Vocabulary Words

- detail
- expand
- improve

Materials

- chart paper
- writing paper
- first drafts of student writing
- teacher-selected nonfiction text

Preparation Note: Prior to the lesson, students should have worked on writing a first draft on any topic of the teachers' or students' choosing. Students should have a teacher-provided topic and at least three facts about the topic in their writing.

Procedures

Model

1. Write the following sentences on a sheet of chart paper:
   - *The baby slept.*
   - *The baby ate food.*
   - *The baby played.*

2. Have students read the sentences aloud with you.

3. Write the following words on a separate sheet of chart paper: *who, what, when, where, why,* and *how.* Explain to students that asking these questions will help improve a sentence, which helps the reader better understand the topic.

4. Begin with the first sentence, emphasizing the question word at the beginning. Tell students that as you read the sentence, you wonder about questions such as:
   - *Where* did the baby sleep?
   - *What* did the baby sleep with?
   - *How* long did the baby sleep?

5. Model answering the questions by adding detail to the sentence. For example:
   - The baby slept *in the crib.*
   - The baby slept *with the pacifier in her mouth.*
   - The baby slept *for three hours.*

Expanding Details *(cont.)*

6. Continue with the second and third sentences in the same way. Invite students to ask questions about what they wonder and then answer the questions by expanding the sentences. Record their sentences on a sheet of chart paper.

Apply/Analyze

7. Tell students that they will be doing a strategy called *Just Say It.* (For detailed information on this strategy, see page 17.) Depending on students' abilities, you may wish to complete this activity as a whole group using various student writing. Students can still discuss adding details with their partners.

8. Put students into pairs. Have the partners face each other and identify one as Partner *A* and the other as Partner *B.*

9. Distribute student writing samples that were collected prior to the lesson. Have Partner *A* share his or her writing with Partner *B.*

10. Provide Partner *B* 30 seconds to respond to the writing of Partner *A.* Encourage students to help provide more detail to the writing by expanding the details. Partner *A* should listen attentively.

11. Have partners switch roles and allow Partner *B* to share his or her writing and Partner *A* to respond.

Evaluate/Create

12. Have students return to their desks to revise their writing by adding details to improve the information they provide, based on the feedback their partners gave them.

13. Allow partners to come back together to share the revised writing if more response is needed.

14. Provide students with a teacher-selected nonfiction text. Have students work individually or with partners to choose a sentence or sentences to analyze. Ask students to identify ways the author answered questions to improve the reader's understanding of the information. Have students determine questions that are answered in each sentence.

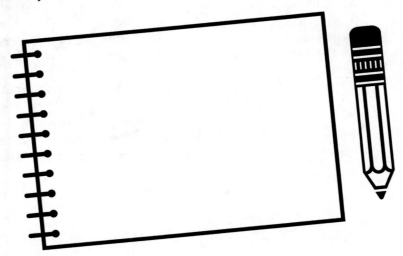

Adding Three Numbers

Brain-Powered Strategy	Standard
Just Say It	Solve word problems that call for addition of three whole numbers whose sum is less than or equal to 20

Vocabulary Words	Materials
• addition • equal to • less than • sum • whole number	• *Adding Three Numbers* (page 132) • chart paper

Procedures

Model

1. Write the problem *3 + 2 =* on the board. Ask students to name the sum.

2. Have students explain how they solved the problem. Try to solicit as many different strategies students used as possible.

3. Explain to students that *3 + 2* is an example of adding two numbers together, and that they will practice adding three numbers together.

4. Write the problem *3 + 2 + 1 =* on the board.

5. Write the steps for solving the problem on a sheet of chart paper as follows or using a different strategy of your choosing:

   Step 1: Add the first two numbers and write the sum. (Draw an arrow to show adding the first two numbers.)

   Step 2: Circle the far right number. (So you don't forget about it!)

   Step 3: Add the far right number to the sum of the first two numbers.

   Step 4: Write the sum.

6. Model several more problems using these steps. You may wish to model problems both vertically and horizontally.

Adding Three Numbers (cont.)

Apply/Analyze

7. Tell students that they will be doing an activity called *Just Say It*. (For detailed information on this strategy, see page 17.)

8. Group students into pairs. Have the two students face each other and identify one as Partner *A* and the other as Partner *B*.

9. Have Partner *A* explain how to find the sum when adding three numbers. Partner *B* should listen attentively.

10. Provide Partner *B* 30 seconds to respond or add more detail to what Partner *A* said. Partner *A* should listen attentively.

11. Have partners switch roles and allow Partner *B* to explain how to solve the problems to Partner *A*.

Evaluate/Create

12. Distribute the *Adding Three Numbers* activity sheet (page 132) to students.

13. Ask students to solve the equations for problems 1–5. Have students create their own equations for problem 6. Display the chart with steps to solve the problems for students to reference.

14. Have students check the answers to problems 1–5 with their partners. Have partners solve problem 6 of each other's papers.

Name: _____   Date: _____

Adding Three Numbers

Directions: Solve the problems below. Use the steps discussed in class.

1. 4 + 3 + 2 =

_____

_____

_____

2. 3 + 1 + 3 =

_____

_____

_____

3. 1 + 2 + 3 =

_____

_____

4. 3 + 2 + 2 =

_____

_____

_____

5. 1 + 4 + 2 =

_____

_____

_____

6. Make up a three-digit addition problem. Have a partner solve it.

_____

_____

_____

What Do You Observe?

Brain-Powered Strategy	**Standard**
Just Say It	Knows that learning can come from careful observation and simple experiments

Vocabulary Words	**Materials**
• observation • senses	• *Observation Recording Sheet* (page 135) • chart paper • apple or other piece of fruit

Preparation Note: Prior to the lesson, determine an experiment or an item for students to base observations on. Divide a sheet of chart paper into five sections such as on the *Observation Recording Sheet* activity sheet (page 135). Write the word *see* in the top box, but do not write the other senses in the remaining boxes until Step 4 in the lesson. Additionally, cut up the selected fruit so all students can sample a small portion. **Note:** Be aware of students' allergies.

Procedures

Model

1. Display the piece of fruit. Ask students to describe what they see. Record students' responses on the previously prepared chart paper.

2. Explain to students that when they describe what they see, they are making an observation.

3. Explain to students that there are many ways to make observations. Tell students that scientists use all of their senses to make observations, not just what they see.

4. Review with students the five senses. Write the other senses on the previously created senses table.

5. Allow students to make observations of the piece of fruit again, this time using all the senses. Remember to check for food allergies before having students eat any foods in the classroom.

6. Record students' responses on the chart paper.

What Do You Observe? *(cont.)*

Apply/Analyze

7. Tell students that they will be doing a strategy called *Just Say It*. (For detailed information on this strategy, see page 17.)

8. Group students into pairs. Have the two students face each other and identify one as Partner *A* and the other as Partner *B*.

9. Have Partner *A* make as many observations as possible in 30 seconds. Partner *B* should listen attentively.

10. Provide Partner *B* 30 seconds to respond or add more detail to what Partner *A* said. Partner *A* should listen attentively.

11. Have partners switch roles, and allow Partner *B* to make additional observations for 30 seconds.

Evaluate/Create

12. Distribute the *Observation Recording Sheet* activity sheet to students.

13. Allow students time to record ideas that were shared among partners. Students can draw or write their observations. Invite several partners to share their observations aloud with the whole class.

14. Have students look at a pencil or another object they all have access to at their desks. Then, hold a pencil as far across the room from students as possible. Ask students to determine how their observations change when they observe something far away versus close by. Allow students to share their ideas and rationales.

Name: _____   Date: _____

Observation Recording Sheet

Directions: Record the observations you made below.

👁 **See**	
👂 **Hear**	👄 **Taste**
👃 **Smell**	✋ **Touch**

Narrative Writing

Brain-Powered Strategy

Show It with Dough!

Standard

Write narratives in which they recount two or more appropriately sequenced events, include some details regarding what happened, use temporal words to signal event order, and provide some sense of closure

Vocabulary Words

- closure
- details
- events
- narrative
- temporal words

Materials

- *No-Cook Dough Recipe* (page 138)
- *A Fun Recess* (page 139)
- chart paper
- cardboard

Preparation Note: Prior to the lesson, create molding dough for students using the *No-Cook Dough Recipe* (page 138). Divide it into enough portions for each student to have some.

Procedures

Model

1. Tell students a little story about some related events that the class experienced earlier in the morning. For example, "Our class got ready for learning. First, we walked into the classroom. Second, we put our backpacks away. Next, we got our pencils out. Then, we were ready to learn."

2. Explain to students that the story you told is called a *narrative,* and it tells about some related events.

3. Display and discuss the writing prompt on the *A Fun Recess* activity sheet (page 139) to students. Explain to students that they will write about related events that happened to make recess fun.

4. Write the word *recess* on the board. Ask students to brainstorm the things they did at recess. Record students' ideas on a sheet of chart paper.

5. Discuss the importance of the sequence of events and words that will help tell the order. Post a list of transition words for students to reference as they discuss and write (e.g., *first, next, then, last, finally*).

6. Provide students with a frame for writing their narratives, as needed. For example: *I had a fun recess. First, _____. Then, _____. Finally, _____.*

7. Model responding to the prompt by writing about a fun recess. Think aloud as you incorporate sequencing the events and adding details to your writing.

Narrative Writing *(cont.)*

Apply/Analyze

8. Tell students that they will be doing a strategy called *Show It with Dough!* (For detailed information on this strategy, see page 18.)

9. Distribute dough and cardboard to each student. Ask students to use the dough as a prewriting tool. Have them mold the dough on top of the cardboard to show what they did at recess. Provide time for students to work.

10. Divide students into groups of three to four. Have each student share his or her model with the other students in the group while telling the story about what happened at recess.

11. Have students who are listening respond to the story by asking questions to elicit details in the student story telling.

12. Allow time for each student in the group to present his or her model. Have students, who are listening to the presentations, identify a temporal word the sharing student used during the presentation.

Evaluate/Create

13. Distribute *A Fun Recess* activity sheet to each student.

14. Reread the prompt with students, and remind them to write their responses while keeping in mind the feedback their groups gave when they were sharing.

15. Allow students to share their finished writing with the same groups so students can hear how their feedback was incorporated into the writing.

16. Have students set their dough model and writing on their desks. Allow time for students to rotate around the room to view the models and read the student writing.

No-Cook Dough Recipe

Teacher Directions: Use the recipe below to make dough.

Ingredients

☑ 1 cup flour

☑ $\frac{3}{8}$ cup salt

☑ $\frac{3}{8}$ cup hot tap water

☑ food coloring *(optional)*

Steps

1. Combine the flour and salt in a medium-size bowl.

2. Pour in the hot water and stir well.

3. Knead the dough for at least five minutes, working in food coloring if desired.

Note: Depending on the thickness of the dough, air-drying can take between one and five days. The dough will keep for up to a week when refrigerated in plastic bags or sealed containers.

Name: _____   Date: _____

A Fun Recess

....

Directions: Read the prompt. Write a response.
Then, draw a picture to represent your response.

Prompt: Write about what you did on the playground.

_____

_ _

_____

_ _

_____

_ _

_____

Plant Parts

Brain-Powered Strategy	**Standard**
Show It with Dough!	Knows that plants and animals have features that help them live in different environments

Vocabulary Words

- features
- flower
- leaves
- roots
- stem

Materials

- *No-Cook Dough Recipe* (page 138)
- *Plant Parts Diagram* (page 142)
- chart paper
- cardboard
- grade-level nonfiction texts on a particular plant or habitat

Preparation Note: Prior to the lesson, create molding dough for students using the *No-Cook Dough Recipe* (page 138). Divide it into enough portions for each student to have some.

Procedures

Model

1. Point to the following parts of your body and have students name them:

   - eyes
   - ears
   - nose

2. Tell students that each body part also has a function. Have students name the functions of each body part (e.g., eyes are for seeing).

3. Explain to students that just like the body, plants have different parts and functions.

4. Draw a diagram of a plant on a sheet of chart paper, one part at a time. Discuss the function of each plant part:

part	function
roots	bring water into the plant
stem	holds the leaves and brings the water up the plant
leaves	make food for the plant
flowers	make the seeds

Plant Parts *(cont.)*

Apply/Analyze

5. Tell students that they will be doing a strategy called *Show It with Dough!* (For detailed information on this strategy, see page 18.)

6. Distribute dough and cardboard to students.

7. Ask students to mold a model that includes all the features of a plant. Keep the chart paper with the plant parts displayed for students to reference as they create their model.

8. Ask students to share their plant models with a partner. Students can give one another feedback about features that were modeled well and features that may be missing. Allow students additional time to work on their models, as needed.

Evaluate/Create

9. Distribute the *Plant Parts Diagram* activity sheet (page 142) to students. Ask students to label the plant features and name the function of each one. Use students' labels and descriptions of functions to assess student understanding of the concept.

10. Provide students with a grade-level nonfiction text on a particular plant or habitat. Have students read the text and determine which part or parts of a plant help the plant survive and how.

Name: _____   Date: _____

Plant Parts Diagram

Directions: Read the function for each plant part. Then, label the part.

These make the seeds.

_____
- - - - - - - - - - - - - - -
_____

These make food for the plant.

_____
- - - - - - - - - - - - - - -
_____

This holds the leaves and brings the water up to the plant.

_____
- - - - - - - - - - - - - - -
_____

These bring water into the plant.

_____
- - - - - - - - - - - - - - -
_____

Map It Out

Brain-Powered Strategy

Show It with Dough!

Standard

Knows that places can be defined in terms of their predominant human and physical characteristics

Vocabulary Words

- geography
- hill
- mountain
- plain
- valley

Materials

- *No-Cook Dough Recipe* (page 138)
- globe or map
- chart paper
- cardboard
- index cards
- drawing paper

Preparation Note: Prior to the lesson, create molding dough for students using the *No-Cook Dough Recipe* (page 138). Divide it into enough portions for each student to have some.

Procedures

Model

1. Display a globe or map. Have students identify the land and water.

2. Tell students that *geography* is the study of the shape of the land and water.

3. Draw a horizontal line on the board or on a sheet of chart paper. Tell students that land that is flat is called a *plain*. Write the word under the line.

4. Continue to draw and describe the shape of other land features such as *hill*, *mountain*, and *valley*. Label each picture. Leave the drawings available for students to reference as they work.

Apply/Analyze

5. Tell students that they will be doing a strategy called *Show It with Dough!* (For detailed information on this strategy, see page 18.)

6. Distribute dough and cardboard to students. Ask students to choose a land feature to model with the dough on top of the cardboard. Provide students time to work.

7. Place an index card in front of each model. Have students stand up and rotate one student to the left. On the index card, have students draw what they see on the model.

8. Repeat Steps 6–7. Encourage students to create different land features each time.

Map It Out *(cont.)*

Evaluate/Create

9. Distribute more cardboard to students. Ask students to create a map that has at least two geographic landforms on it. Students can choose their own two features or identify two specific features that should be included.

10. Ask students to display their maps on their desks. Have the class rotate around the room to view the other students' maps.

11. Have students return to their own maps. Ask them to label the geographic features on their maps in pencil. Review students' labeled maps to assess student progress with the lesson concept. Take anecdotal notes, as needed.

Counting

Brain-Powered Strategy	Standard
Reverse, Reverse!	Count to 120, starting at any number less than 120
Vocabulary Words	**Materials**
• counting • reverse	• *Counting Mat* (page 147) • number line or number grid

Procedures

Model

1. Draw a number line from 1–30 on the board. Have students practice counting to thirty aloud with you. Point to the numbers on the number line as students say them aloud.

2. Practice counting to 30 several more times. Each time, have students use a different voice such as a baby voice, an opera voice, and a papa bear voice.

3. Ask students what number comes after 30. Tell students that before they can continue to count, you will add on to the number line. Add a few more numbers to the number line you wrote on the board. Then, make the connection between the number line you drew and the number line or number grid in your classroom.

4. Continue counting numbers greater than 30. As you point to each number, say the number aloud and have students repeat the number.

5. Begin a new number line beginning from 100. Have students practice counting aloud to 120 on the number line or number grid as you point to each number. Practice several times, using various voices as suggested in Step 2.

6. Choose a number in the middle of the number line. Have students practice counting forward from that number. Point to the numbers on the number line or number grid to provide support, as needed.

Counting *(cont.)*

Apply/Analyze

7. Tell students that they will be doing a strategy called *Reverse, Reverse!* (For detailed information on this strategy, see page 19.)

8. Gather students together to form a circle. Select one student to be the judge, or you can be the judge.

9. Have the first student begin counting at 1 (or any other number you designate). Continue having students count in a clockwise direction. The next student says the next number, and so on. If a student makes a mistake in the number sequence, reverse the direction so the direction is now counterclockwise.

10. An alternative is to have students reverse the direction of counting each time the teacher says, "Reverse!" Practice counting by twos, fives, and tens following the same procedures.

11. Play continues until a predetermined amount of time, number of times around the circle, or a specific number is reached in counting (e.g., 120).

Evaluate/Create

12. Distribute the *Counting Mat* activity sheet (page 147) to students. Designate a number for students to write in the first box.

13. Have students continue to write numbers from that starting number until all the boxes are filled. Have students work individually or with partners depending on the time of year and students' abilities.

14. Arrange students into pairs. Ask students to determine if the numbers get larger or smaller when reading to the right/left and how they know. Group two sets of partners together, so there are now four students in a group. Have each share their answers and rationales.

$$5 + 8 =$$
$$6 + 9 =$$
$$1\,0 - 5 =$$

Name: _____   Date: _____

Counting Mat

....

Directions: Practice counting and writing numbers. Listen to your teacher for what number to write in the first box.

Animal Types

Brain-Powered Strategy	Standard
Reverse, Reverse!	Knows that plants and animals have features that help them live in different environments

Vocabulary Words

- bird
- insect
- mammal
- reptile

Materials

- *Animal Groups* (page 150)
- chart paper
- photographs of various animals
- crayons

Procedures

Model

1. Ask students to think of their favorite animals. Have students turn to a partner and name their favorites.

2. Have each student share aloud his or her favorite animal. Record student responses on a sheet of chart paper.

3. Review with students the various types of animal groups the class has been studying and the features of each group. Make a chart that lists the various features of each animal group. For example:

Animal	Features
mammals	have hair or fur, give live birth, mothers feed babies milk
birds	have feathers, most fly, have two legs, lay eggs
reptiles	have scales, lay eggs, cold-blooded
insects	have three body parts, six legs, lay eggs, many fly

4. Display photographs of animals, one at a time. Ask students to share with a partner which animal group each animal belongs to and why. Call on students to share their answers and discuss as a group, if needed.

5. Return to the list of animals generated by students in Step 2. Work together as a class to identify the animal groups each animal belongs to.

Animal Types *(cont.)*

Apply/Analyze

6. Tell students that they will be doing a strategy called *Reverse, Reverse!* (For detailed information on this strategy, see page 19.)

7. Gather students together to form a circle. Select one student to be the judge, or you can be the judge.

8. Name an animal group (e.g., mammals). Have the first student begin by naming an animal in that group as well as a feature that helps that animal survive in its environment. Continue around the circle in a clockwise direction. The next student says another animal, and so on. If a student cannot think of an animal or repeats an animal already named, reverse the direction so the direction is now counterclockwise.

9. As students play, record their ideas on a sheet of chart paper. The animal group can be changed each time the direction of play is reversed in order to add excitement to the game.

10. Play continues until a predetermined amount of time or until students cannot think of any more animals.

Evaluate/Create

11. Distribute the *Animal Groups* activity sheet (page 150) to students. Have students name one characteristic of each animal group and draw one animal that belongs in each group.

12. Arrange students into groups of three to four. Ask students to choose one person's activity sheet. Have the group work together to name a similar characteristic for the animals drawn on the page. For example, students could name body coverings or types of food eaten for all four animals.

Name: _____   Date: _____

Animal Groups

Directions: Tell one thing you know about each animal group. Draw an animal that belongs in each group.

Mammal	**Bird**
Insect	**Reptile**

Map Maker

Brain-Powered Strategy	Standard
Reverse, Reverse!	Understands the characteristics and uses of maps, globes, and other geographic tools and technologies

Vocabulary Words

- compass
- element
- key
- map
- symbols

Materials

- *Make a Map* (page 153)
- chart paper
- samples of maps and globes
- crayons

Procedures

Model

1. Draw a square (or the shape of your classroom) on chart paper. Tell students that this is a map of your classroom.

2. Ask students to help name the items in your classroom. Draw a quick picture of each item on the map in the correct place.

3. Explain to students that you will complete this map after looking at some maps that have already been made.

4. Display maps and globes where students can see them.

5. Point out, name, and describe the various features of maps and globes including the following:

   - title
   - compass rose
   - map key
   - symbols
   - any other features shown on the maps you have

6. List and briefly describe on chart paper the features of maps and globes as you discuss them.

7. Return to the classroom map created in Steps 1 and 2. Complete the map by adding the features listed in Step 5.

Map Maker *(cont.)*

Apply/Analyze

8. Tell students that they will be doing a strategy called *Reverse, Reverse!* (For detailed information on this strategy, see page 19.)

9. Gather students together to form a circle. Select one student to be the judge, or you can be the judge.

10. Have the first student begin by naming an element of a map or globe (e.g., compass, legend, title). Continue around the circle in a clockwise direction. The next student says another element, and so on. If a student cannot think of an element or repeats an element already named, reverse the direction so the direction is now counterclockwise.

11. As students play, record their ideas on a sheet of chart paper.

12. Play continues until a predetermined amount of time or until students cannot think of any more elements.

Evaluate/Create

13. Distribute the *Make a Map* activity sheet (page 153) to students.

14. Have students create their own maps by including the elements that they named and you listed on the chart paper. Leave the chart paper displayed for students to reference.

15. Have students work with partners to compare their maps. Ask student pairs to discuss questions for each feature such as:

- Where did you place your compass rose and why?

- Does it matter/not matter where the compass rose was placed?

- Does having the compass rose in a particular place make the map easier/harder to read and why?

Name: _____   Date: _____

Make a Map

Directions: Create your own map. Be sure to include a title and the key elements of a map.

References Cited

Anderson, Lorin and David Krathwohl (Eds.). 2001. *Taxonomy for Learning, Teaching, and Assessing: A Revision of Bloom's Taxonomy of Educational Objectives.* Boston, MA: Pearson Education Group.

Bloom, Benjamin (Ed.). 1956. *Taxonomy of Educational Objectives.* New York: David McKay Company.

Covington, Martin V. 2000. "Goal Theory, Motivation, and School Achievement: An Integrative Review." Retrieved from http://www2.csdm.qc.ca/SaintEmile/bernet/annexes/ASS6826/Covington2000.pdf.n.

Csikszentmihalyi, Mihaly. 1996. *Creativity: Flow and the Psychology of Discovery and Invention.* New York: HarperCollins.

Doidge, Norman. 2007. *The Brain That Changes Itself: Stories of Personal Triumph from the Frontiers of Brain Science.* New York, NY: Penguin Books.

Eldridge, L. Laura, Steven Engel, Michael Zeineh, S. Y. Bookheimer, and B. J. Knowlton. 2005. In *Mind, Brain, and Education: Neuroscience Implications for the Classroom,* edited by David A. Sousa. Bloomington, IN: Solution Tree.

Harris, Bryan, and Cassandra Goldberg. 2012. *75 Quick and Easy Solutions to Common Classroom Disruptions.* Florence, KY: Routledge.

Hunter, Madeline. 1993. *Enhancing Teaching.* Upper Saddle River, NJ: Prentice Hall.

Huntington's Outreach Program for Education, at Stanford (HOPES). 2010. "Neuroplasticity." http://www.stanford.edu/group/hopes/cgi-bin/wordpress/2010/06/neuroplasticity.

Immordino-Yang, Mary H. and Matthias Faeth. 2010. "The Role of Emotion and Skilled Intuition in Learning." In *Mind, Brain, and Education: Neuroscience Implications for the Classroom,* edited by David A. Sousa, 69–83. Bloomington, IN: Solution Tree.

McCombs, Barbara L. 1997 "Understanding the Keys to Motivation to Learn." Retrieved from http://incolor.inetnebr.com/fadams/motivation_exercise.htm.

Medina, John. 2008. *Brain Rules: 12 Principles for Surviving and Thriving at Work, Home, and School.* Seattle, WA: Pear Press.

Merzenich, Michael. 2013. *Soft-Wired: How the New Science of Brain Plasticity Can Change Your Life.* San Francisco, CA: Parnassus Publishing, LLC.

Overbaugh, Richard C. and Lynn Schultz. n.d. "Bloom's Taxonomy." Retrieved from http://ww2.odu.edu/educ/roverbau/Bloom/blooms_taxonomy.htm.

Ratey, John J. 2008. *Spark: The Revolutionary New Science of Exercise and the Brain.* New York, NY: Little, Brown and Company.

Roth, LaVonna. 2012. *Brain-Powered Strategies to Engage All Learners.* Huntington Beach, CA: Shell Education.

References Cited *(cont.)*

Schenck, Jeb. 2005 . "Teaching to the Brain." Retrieved from
http://www.aa.edu/ftpimages/109/download/TeachingToTheBrain_Schenck.pdf.

Sousa, David A. 2006. *How the Brain Learns,* 3rd ed. Bloomington, IN: Solution Tree.

Thomas, Alice and Glenda Thorne. 2009. "How to Increase Higher Order Thinking."
Retrieved from http://www.cdl.org/resourcelibrary/articles/HOT.php?type=subject&id=18.

Van Tassell, Gene. 2004. "Neural Pathway Development."
Retrieved from http://www.brains.org/path.htm.

Vaynman, Shoshanna, Zhe Ying, and Fernando Gomez-Pinilla. 2004. "Hippocampal BDNF
Mediates the Efficacy of Exercise on Synaptic Plasticity and Cognition." *European Journal
of Neuroscience* 20: 2580–2590.

Vermillion, Francesca. 2010. "The Interior Parts of the Brain." Retrieved from
http://www.livestrong.com/article/92897-interior-parts-brain/.

Webb, Norman L. 2005. "Alignment, Depth of Knowledge, and Change." Presented at the
50th annual meeting of the Florida Educational Research Association, Miami, FL. Abstract
retrieved from http://facstaff.wcer.wisc.edu/normw/MIAMI%20FLORIDA%20FINAL%20
slides%2011-15-05.pdf.

Wiggins, Grant and Jay McTighe. 2005. *Understanding by Design,* 2nd ed. Upper Saddle
River, NJ: Prentice Hall.

Willis, Judy. 2008. *How Your Child Learns Best: Brain-Friendly Strategies You Can Use to
Ignite Your Child's Learning and Increase School Success.* Naperville, IL: Sourcebooks,
Inc.

Wolfe, Pat and Ron Brandt. 1998. In *How the Brain Learns,* 3rd ed, edited by David A.
Sousa. Bloomington, IN: Solution Tree.

Wyoming School Health and Physical Education. 2001. "Standards, Assessment, and
Beyond." Retrieved May 25, 2006 from http://www.uwyo.edu/wyhpenet.

Contents of the Digital Resource CD

Pages	Lesson	Filename
29–43	Vowel Sort	vowelsort.pdf
44–57	Attributes of Shapes	attributesofshapes.pdf
58–61	Sink or Float?	sinkorfloat.pdf
62–64	Characters: Same and Different	sameanddifferent.pdf
65–67	In My Opinion	inmyopinion.pdf
68–69	Is Bigger Better?	isbiggerbetter.pdf
70–72	Nouns and Verbs	nounsandverbs.pdf
73–76	Wonderful Weather	wonderfulweather.pdf
77–80	Life Long Ago	lifelongago.pdf
81–88	There Is Support	thereissupport.pdf
89–96	Elaborate with Details	elaboratewithdetails.pdf
97–105	Number Representations	numberrepresentations.pdf
106–113	Goods and Services	goodsandservices.pdf
114–116	What Does It Mean?	whatdoesitmean.pdf
117–124	It Represents the U.S.	itrepresentstheus.pdf
125–127	Character Connections	characterconnections.pdf
128–129	Expanding Details	expandingdetails.pdf
130–132	Adding Three Numbers	addingthreenumbers.pdf
133–135	What Do You Observe?	whatdoyouobserve.pdf
136–139	Narrative Writing	narrativewriting.pdf
140–142; 138	Plant Parts	plantparts.pdf
143–144; 138	Map It Out	mapitout.pdf
145–147	Counting	counting.pdf
148–150	Animal Types	animaltypes.pdf
151–153	Map Maker	mapmaker.pdf

Page(s)	Additional Resource	Filename
12–19	Strategy Overviews	strategyoverviews.pdf
25–27	Standards	standards.pdf
138	No-Cook Dough Recipe	doughrecipe.pdf
72; 75; 79	ABC Professor Notes Activity Sheet	abcprofessornotes.pdf
NA	Enlarged Activity Cards (This folder contains the following: topicdetailcards.pdf, definitioncards.pdf sentencecards.pdf, fivewcards.pdf, numbercards.pdf, symbolcards.pdf, and goodservicescards.pdf)	Enlarged Cards

Notes

Notes

Notes

Notes